Dreams
and Sexuality

Dreams
and Sexuality

Interpreting Your
Sexual Dreams

Pam Spurr Ph.D.

Illustrated by Anthea Toorchen

Sterling Publishing Co., Inc.
New York

For Nick forever

AN EDDISON•SADD EDITION
Edited, designed and produced by
Eddison Sadd Editions Limited
St Chad's House
148 King's Cross Road
London WC1X 9DH

Library of Congress
Cataloging-in-Publication Data Available

10 9 8 7 6 5 4 3 2 1

Published in 2001 by Sterling Publishing Company Inc.
387 Park Avenue South, New York, N.Y. 10016

Distributed in Canada by Sterling Publishing
c/o Canadian Manda Group,
One Atlantic Avenue, Suite 105
Toronto, Ontario, Canada M6K 3E7

Distributed in Australia by
Capricorn Link (Australia) Pty Ltd
P.O. Box 6651, Baulkham Hills, Business Centre
NSW 2153, Australia

Phototypeset in Deepdene and ExPonto using
QuarkXPress on Apple Macintosh
Origination by Atlas Mediacom (S) Pte Ltd, Singapore
Printed in Spain by Grafo, S.A. Industrias Graficas

Sterling paperback edition ISBN 0-8069-5873-1
Sterling hardback edition ISBN 0-8069-5077-3

Contents

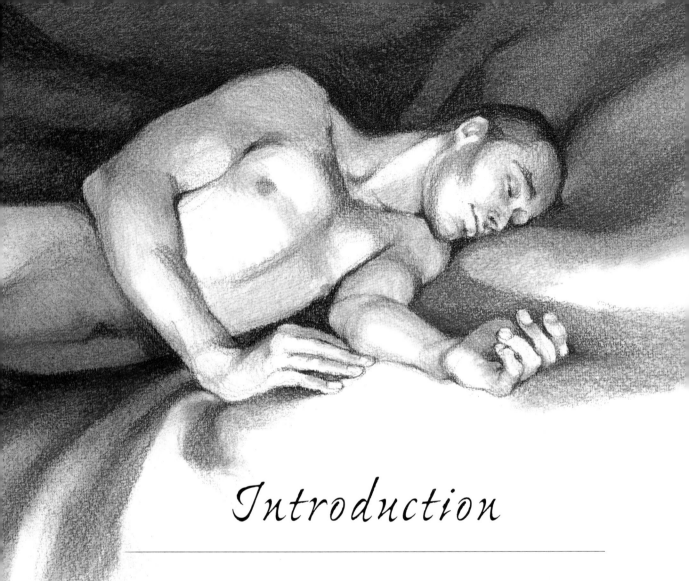

Introduction

Have you ever woken from a dream feeling inexplicably anxious and yet sexually charged? Or have you felt embarrassed because you dreamed that you slept with your boss? Many of our dreams hold the key to a fuller understanding of our sexual selves. This practical book shows you how to explore your dreams to learn more about your sexual needs, desires, feelings and attitudes. By nurturing your sexual self you will gradually reduce any negative sexual attitudes or inhibitions, increasing your sexual confidence and improving your overall sense of well-being. This in turn will lead to more enjoyable and fulfilling emotional and sexual relationships.

The first section of the book – Practical Interpretation – shows you how to set about exploring your dreams, highlighting the importance of approaching dream interpretation with an open and positive mind. It also provides specially devised sensual exercises to help you shape your dreams and develop your sexual awareness.

At the heart of the book is the Dream Finder. This section sets out a wide range of sexual dream case studies that illustrate myriad feelings, dilemmas and problems, and offers insightful interpretation of each. Categorized into overtly sexual, veiled sexual and absurd sexual dreams, the description and analysis of each case study provides a starting point for the exploration of your own dreams, providing insights into their possible meanings. Each dream study is accompanied by practical advice that will help resolve the inner conflicts or relationship issues raised by the dream analysis, together with a sensual exercise, questionnaire or details of related symbolism.

Finally, the Dream Directory provides a quick reference to the wide range of symbolism commonly found in sexual dreams, many of which are not overtly sexual. A range of possible interpretations are given, according to the feelings that accompany the dream images.

The Purpose of Dreaming

As we spend a full third of our lives asleep, what goes on during this fascinating and complex process should be of great interest to us. When people consider the number of hours involved, they start to wonder why they are asleep so much of their lives. Are there mysteries they should understand and explore, they muse? What is the whole sleeping process all about? In particular, they begin to wonder about their dreams.

The very nature of our dream life ignites an interest in most people. Everyone dreams, and most people recall either some of their dreams images – passages or portions of their dreams – or entire dreams from time to time. Some of our earliest memories often contain dream images. These range from the childhood nightmare that scared the living daylights out of us (and made us feel compelled to creep into our parents' bed for comfort!) to the joy we experienced while soaring above the clouds in wonderful fantastical dreams. As adults our dream life may be every bit as rich and varied as our childhood dream life.

Dreams contain many different elements. They range from potent and defined images that reflect the facets of our life to complex, multi-layered moods without actual images. Sometimes we dream of absurd scenarios that amaze us on waking. We wonder how our minds created such imagery. Our mind at night seems to become one great creative and fertile garden of thoughts, feelings and experiences.

THE DEVELOPMENT OF YOUR PERSONALITY

How did you come to be the unique person you are with all your individual traits, your own ways of relating to others and your overall dynamic nature that carries you through life? Your personality is the essence of your essential self. It reflects the distillation of all your experiences that you bring to life's encounters. This question about the development of personality forms the backdrop to understanding more about yourself and your dream life. Every aspect of your personality – emotional, social, intellectual or cognitive, and sexual – is inextricably linked with the others. One area cannot develop in any way without having some kind of effect on another.

For example, perhaps you grew up in a family where emotions were kept on a tight rein. Your parents never argued with each other – they would quietly sort out or ignore their differences – and they never showed much joy or excitement either. They preferred a calm, controlled household, and you were raised to fit in with this. Consequently, you took this sort of emotional 'style' to school with you. You were one of the quieter pupils who did not get particularly excited when, for example, the science teacher concocted an unusual experiment that made some pupils gasp. And your cognitive development was controlled and steady rather like your emotions. The one affected the other. Your social development was also affected. Your peer group

viewed you as a steady, reliable friend but not necessarily the life and soul of the party. And, later on, your lovers generally viewed you as a good companion and considerate lover, although not electric in bed.

I believe the best way of describing the development of personality, and how the main elements of it interact, is to use the analogy of the river. The water of a river is best likened to your emotional development. It churns and rushes, plunges and then gently flows by turn, depending on the twists and turns the 'river' (your life) takes. The river of your life began with your parents, with their beliefs and ways of interacting with the world. As the river matures through childhood, and you

absorb your parents' sexual attitudes, too, your emotional development comes to include your sexual development. In the midst of a passionate sexual affair the waters of your river gush violently. Then, when you enjoy the quieter moments in a longer-term relationship with a lover, the water flows more gently .

The riverbanks are analogous to your social development. As your personality develops, so too does the instruction you receive – from your parents when young and from others as you grow older – in the subtleties of social interaction. Your social learning, or the development of the banks of your river, helps to contain the churning emotional waters when you are upset and shape the bubbling waters that happiness and passion bring.

Of course, some people never really learn the subtle nuances of social interaction and continually upset others as they move through life, with their emotions spilling out all over the banks of a river that never properly formed.

The huge variety of life in the water, together with the stones and plants that the river contains, symbolize your cognitive development. As your personality encounters obstructions it learns to cope with hurdles and challenges: you learn to do a job, study or solve the problems life throws at you. Your cognitive development interacts with your emotional waters and is contained by the riverbanks,

the socialization process. The three distinct parts of your personality – banks, waters and elements – together form the whole system of development for your entire personality.

Your dream life reflects every aspect of your personality – your essential self – giving clues as to what is important to you at that time. Some dreams reflect social issues or dilemmas encountered in your interaction with others. For example, if you were concerned about whether you said the right thing to someone in a social situation recently, the whole incident may come flooding back to you in dream images. Some dreams reflect cognitive issues. For example, you may experience an anxiety dream that ties in with your recent struggle with a difficult task at work. Other dreams reflect sexual and emotional issues: the deeper passions of your sexual experiences, some lingering doubts from past relationships or the wish fulfilment of your sexual fantasy life.

THE SLEEP CYCLE

Before we begin the wonderful journey of learning about our sexual dreams, it is important to understand the process of sleep. Researchers have pondered the question, 'Why should we spend a third of our lives asleep?' for as long as there has been interest in human consciousness. Until relatively recently it was accepted that we need this 'time out' from consciousness to replenish our batteries and prepare us for the vigours of the day ahead. Although this may be an important reason for sleeping, most scientists now agree that the main purpose of sleeping may be to allow dreaming!

Sleep studies have demonstrated that the brain undergoes many discreet transformations during the sleep cycle. The electrical activity measured during these changes are seen as a series of stages. As you begin to relax, feeling drowsy and less alert, you are entering Stage One sleep. You are still semi-conscious of your surroundings. As you gradually fall into an unconscious sleep state you pass through Stage Two sleep and then Stage Three sleep: this takes approximately twenty to thirty minutes. After this you begin to progress into Stage Four sleep. This is called slow-wave sleep: it is the deepest level of sleep, during which the electrical activity in your brain takes the shape of long, elegant waves of energy.

The sleep cycle lasts for approximately ninety minutes, at the end of which the brain waves change abruptly. Suddenly there appears a burst of electrical brain activity that seems even more lively than the brain activity recorded during waking life! While this takes place, the eye muscles jerk and twitch distinctively, earning this sleep stage the name REM sleep; REM stands for 'rapid eye movement'. REM sleep lasts for approximately twenty minutes and re-emerges at ninety-minute intervals. Sleep experiments have demonstrated that people awoken at this stage in the sleep cycle report that they were dreaming.

During the REM sleep stage the body undergoes 'sleep paralysis': your entire body is paralysed except for your chest, to allow you to breathe, and your eyes, which are moving in this lively fashion. Researchers propose that sleep paralysis is a protective mechanism to stop people from 'acting out' their dreams and potentially harming themselves.

The importance of the REM stage of sleep was only discovered when sleep experiments found that disturbed REM stage sleep resulted in emotional difficulties. Furthermore, research has found that the limbic system, a more primitive part of our brains, goes into overdrive during the REM sleep stage, showing frantic electrical activity.

Sleep specialists believe that the involvement of this primitive portion of our brains allows us to 'process' the events of the day, or experiences of long-standing importance, which have deep emotional meaning for us. This processing allows for our essential self, deep within our subconscious, to mull over issues and possibly arrive at solutions, or emotional turning points, that appear to us in the symbolism of our dreams. At the very least, the images in your dreams are symbols of the experiences and feelings that are registering in the deepest levels of your subconscious. By allowing this process, dreaming appears to play an important role in keeping you emotionally healthy.

DEEPER LEVELS OF CONSCIOUSNESS

Have you ever experienced the sudden re-emergence of an old memory, which you thought you had completely forgotten about, triggered by the occurrence of an event or incident in the present that is somehow similar? Or have you ever experienced an emotion and thought 'I know this feeling!'? Perhaps *déjà vu* – a sense of revisiting something – is a familiar experience with you? All these experiences reveal how much is tucked away from our everyday thoughts. Of course, we could not remember everything that has happened to us all at the same time – our consciousness would be jammed with literally millions of memories. But we do have an enormous potential to store memories of a variety of kinds, from actual events to memories of feelings or sensations.

Just because memories are stored away does not mean that at least some of them do not have a significant effect on our present lifestyle and outlook. A good example is the way people who become romantically involved suddenly have a sense of having known their lover 'all their lives'. This is because subtleties in their lover's behaviour or attitudes reminds them at a deeper level of their own behaviour and attitudes. Usually this reflects similarities in family background and style of relating learned in childhood. This deeper, subconscious level of a person's mind contains a detailed sense of all that has taken place in their life. Although you may be unaware of its existence, this deeper level of consciousness is very important in that it can dictate whether we feel comfortable with a new partner. That comfort, or lack of it, comes from deep in the memory of what we were comfortable with as we were growing up.

The way we relate at a sexual level is another way of demonstrating the impact of this deeper lever of consciousness. Have you ever been in bed with a new lover and found yourself experiencing feelings you have had with previous lovers, even though the new lover seems completely different from the last one in terms of appearance, attitudes and behaviour? A closer analysis would probably reveal that their inherent sexual assumptions learnt in childhood are similar to those of previous lovers.

To take another quite common example, perhaps at the beginning of a new relationship you experience a feeling after lovemaking of guilt or regret, whoever the lover. You wonder why you always have this feeling after sex in the early days. It is the deeper level of your subconscious communicating with you. At some point in your past you received the message that sex was bad, unclean or only good in the context of a long-term relationship. You carry around this memory of what sex 'is' that becomes a 'fact', or part of your present self. It is always there when you embark on a sexual relationship. You may not be consciously aware of it when you first feel attracted to someone. You may not even notice it as the two of you get closer. But once that sexual connection is made your present state of awareness is linked through subconscious mechanisms to hidden memories from your childhood days.

OVERLAPPING LEVELS OF CONSCIOUSNESS

The interaction between conscious and subconscious levels of awareness is complex. There are many ways in which our subconsious affects our conscious behaviour, feelings and choices. In addition to unpleasant memories, or sensations, locked away deep in our long-term memory banks, we may also have positive feelings, or possess unfulfilled desires that we are not consciously aware of most of the time. Both can affect the way we feel sexually in our present lives.

For example, perhaps have had a wonderful sexual relationship at some point in the past. You may not consciously think about it any more but deep down in your subconscious you now have this example, or model, of what you expect from every sexual relationship. Consequently, if a new sexual relationship does not at some level feel right, it is probably because it is not living up to this deeper excellent sexual relationship model, which has become a benchmark for you.

This deeper model may signal directly to your conscious level by presenting it with images from your past, satisfying relationship. You then consciously compare the two and conclude that the present relationship does not match the old in crucial ways. It may signal to you less directly: you may simply have an intuitive feeling that the new relationship is not going to work. Or it may signal to you through your dream life.

Dreams can offer an amazing connection between conscious and subconscious levels of awareness. The rich symbolism of your dreams may spell out a direct message from your inner self – images of your 'ex' bathed in eroticism flood into your dreams, while your new lover is nowhere to be seen. Or your dreams may offer more oblique, veiled symbolism, the meaning of which is only revealed by painstaking analysis. In addition, you may also find yourself resisting a new relationship in subtle, unacknowledged ways. You jeopardize its development by not returning phone calls from your new lover or not allowing physical contact to develop without really knowing why. In this way your subconscious exerts control over your conscious behaviour even if you do not perceive it as such.

Unfulfilled desires locked away in your subconscious may also spur you on to seek out certain sexual activities, encounters or relationships. Sometimes people feel compelled to have sexual relationships with, for example, sexually dominant lovers. They may say that they do not know why they always end up with the same sort of person, but they are undoubtedly influenced by subconscious yearnings that they are not even aware of. Careful exploration of recurring types of behaviour usually reveals early experiences that have led to certain patterns of sexual behaviour later in adult life.

People are often surprised by what is contained in the deeper recesses of their minds and how this affects their lives now. However, when you consider the vast range of human behaviour and complexity of the human mind it should not be so surprising.

THE AIM OF PROTECTIVE MECHANISMS

Your subconscious may sometimes place very direct images in your dreams, or suddenly throw up a memory that connects to your present life, which is startling or disconcerting or even painful to contemplate. At other times, though, your subconscious can break unpleasant news to you slowly, so that the message seeps into your conscious awareness in a measured, non-threatening way. This is a form of protective mechanism. Veiled images in your dreams very often serve this purpose. Slowly you make the connection between the dream images and your waking life. It is a 'dawning' process. The images, exposed in this way, may symbolize a number of things. They may represent deeper longings, sexual frustrations, or anxiety and fear of something at a deeper level.

Another way in which a protective mechanism can work is through the containment of an unhappy experience. In this case, the unhappy memory is repressed by your mind and may appear to have no real effect on you in your waking life. But when you are ready to handle the experience, the subconscious brings the unpleasant memory to your awareness, either through dreams or recollections. Very often this occurs at a time of change or personal growth. At such times people experience vivid dreams that throw up material containing a wealth of symbolism. Or they experience a waking revelation in which a connection is made to the past in a way that sheds light on their present behaviour or relationships.

Your secret garden

To better understand this amazing process, I like to use the analogy of the secret garden of your mind. From the relaxed state just before you fall asleep to the deepest part of your sleep cycle can be seen as a long and winding garden that has depths hidden from view at the outset.

When you are relaxed but still aware, your mind unlatches the first gate into the beginning of your glorious garden. This bright and brilliant garden contains clear and understandable images. As your mind tumbles downwards further away from consciousness, as you fall asleep, you pass through this bright and brilliant garden to the next gate. As you fall deeper into sleep, subsequent gates open to reveal further sections of this lush arena, shedding light on the workings of your mind. Plunging ever more deeply into the secret depths of your garden, the gate latches loosen one after the other and allow you to 'see' into your inner self. The deepest part of the garden is where dreaming takes place, allowing you wonderful glimpses into long-forgotten memories or emotions that are percolating under your consciousness. The garden comes alive with feelings, thoughts and memories that have been tucked away during your waking life.

If you wake at this moment you will fully enjoy the playfulness of your garden. If you wake later in the sleep cycle you may be able to recall only vague or fragmented images from your once-vivid dream. These, though, may be pieced together to recapture the full sense of your dreamscape. People are often astonished by the nature and range of the images they recall from the secret garden of their dreams. These images may help unlock creativity within their relationships, giving them ideas of what they may like to try sexually. Or they may enhance their knowledge of their inner self, allowing self-development and with it, development in their sexual relationships.

Of course, the secret garden of your dream life may contain nightmarish images from time to time. Confronting frightening imagery, which has been hidden behind the gates in the deeper reaches of your garden, may help you move forward in your relationships. Perhaps they deal with problems of an intimate nature, which you have been avoiding for a long time. Nightmares signal to you that some issue is not being dealt with appropriately or even recognized. They may relate to an event, conversation or behaviour that has recently taken place or they may refer to a longstanding issue that has been tucked away far from your consciousness for a very long time.

THE VALUE OF DREAM INTERPRETATION

Whether or not we choose to recognize it, our dream life reflects our inner self. Learning to appreciate the rich symbolism of your secret garden can sometimes provide astonishing insights into your inner self. Our sleeping mind is unfettered by the more rational thoughts presented by the 'inner voice' that operates during our waking hours. This inner voice provides a running dialogue throughout the day. As events take place or thoughts cross your mind, this voice often reacts quite restrictively, particularly when the events or thoughts have some sexual content. Your inner waking voice might ask: 'Is what I'm thinking "right" to think about?' or 'Should I be thinking about this person/topic/issue in this sexual way?' or perhaps 'I can't say that to my lover, it's too embarrassing!' Then, depending on your inner response to such thoughts, you may try to force the issue out of your mind. Consequently, the

'voiceless', sleeping mind provides a comparatively powerful tool to understand ourselves at a deeper emotional level. This is why learning to explore and then interpret your dream life can enrich you as an individual.

EXPLORING YOUR SEXUAL SELF

The practice of dream interpretation may enhance our lives in a number of ways. As we grow older much of the content of our dreams reflects our burgeoning interest in making intimate and sexual connections with others. Sometimes our dreams fulfil heart-felt longings that we have kept secretly to ourselves; sometimes they replay our first forays into sexual activity; and sometimes they paint unbelievable dreamscapes of sensual and erotic content that go far beyond our waking fantasy life. In the process of analysing any of these dreams we may simply enjoy the erotic sensations contained within them.

We may also look to our sexual dreams for new ideas for sexual activity. And we may explore them for revelations of unrecognized desires or frustrations, or to rediscover past issues that we had forgotten but which are , in fact, affecting us now. There are, of course, dreams where the content mystifies us, and where the symbolism may be quite irrelevant. The sleeping mind sometimes strings together images from different aspects of our lives, so that the dreams are actually nonsensical. With such dreams, accurate interpretation may be impossible but analysis of them can still be a pleasant and worthwhile experience.

Exploring your sexual dreams means being prepared to explore your sexual self. Think of your sexual self – what does it mean to you? Does it include the fantasies you sometimes create in a quiet waking moment? Does it mean the way you treat your lover; how far you will push back the boundaries of sexual activity; how you even feel about sex and how 'sexy' you think you are? Perhaps it includes the running dialogue inside your mind that comments on people you find attractive as the day goes by, or notices a gorgeous film star and wonders what they would be like in bed. Yes, all of these and more shape your sexual self, or sexual identity. Your sexuality goes to the core of your inner self. It is an essential part of you and defines how you relate to potential or longstanding partners.

Next, think of all the sexual images that surround you in modern society. You cannot escape the overt sexual imagery in magazines, television, films and books, although you may be only partly aware of the more subtle sexual imagery that exists, particularly in advertising. Our senses are bombarded with these sexual messages. Add to this your internal private world of sexuality – your sexual thoughts, feelings, desires, memories, attitudes, fears and inhibitions – and you will appreciate that sex plays a large part in your conscious life. This mix of sexual images and thoughts influences how you relate to your lover and any potential lovers. And of course many of these sexual stimuli are relegated to your subconscious, where they remain sometimes passive, and other times an active influence on your actions.

So many of our actions concerning our sexual relationships seem at times to be what people describe as 'out of our control', or beyond conscious reasoning. But at some level, whether conscious or unconscious, we choose to act in certain ways even if we feel as though we have been propelled to act in those ways. We wonder about how we came to be with a particular lover. And we think about why we allowed them to do a certain sexual practice but not another, or why we did not enjoy sex one evening but did the next day. In trying to understand ourselves at a sexual level the important question is: 'How can we order and structure this interesting and complex mixture of sexual experience, attitudes and feelings so that we can better understand our sexual selves?'

I believe that the best way to define your sexual self accurately, and then to understand the implications of your definition, is to explore the following four aspects of your sexuality:

1. The way you think about sex
2. The way you feel about sex
3. Your sexual behaviour
4. Your sexual dream life.

Although the first three aspects of your sexual self may seem completely straight-forward, they are not. The way you feel, think and behave in the way you express your sexual self are not always rational. Let me give you an example of someone who longs to have a rich sexual relationship, in which both lovers derive equal pleasure and delight in satisfying each other and themselves. This person thinks that they have met the right person to have such a relationship with. They think they are compatible. They think they find each other mutually attractive. Yet this person, when faced with finally going to bed with their new lover, behaves with timidity. Such contradictions are frequent in sexual relationships, which is one of the reasons why so many people have difficulty in understanding themselves at a sexual level. The conflict between what you are feeling and what you are actually doing can result in sexual tension, frustration or even fear.

When people sense that something is not quite right in the way they are interacting in a sexual relationship, often their thoughts, feelings and behaviour are so confused that they do not know where to start in understanding their difficulties. Looking at the four aspects of your sexuality that I have identified, in order, should help you to start clarifying what is happening in a particular sexual interaction. When you next feel confused about a sexual experience or relationship issue, first make a note of what you *think* about it. Are you thinking that this is not a positive way to behave? Then consider your *feelings*. Are you feeling guilty, frustrated, hurt, unhappy or even angry about the sexual issue? Next look at your actual *behaviour*. Think through what you did step by step. Did you withdraw from lovemaking at a certain point? Or did you say something you regretted? Examining each aspect in detail is a very positive starting point to understanding your sexual self. Exploring the sexual content of your dreams is the final step to understanding your sexual self.

ANALYSING YOUR SEXUAL DREAM LIFE

Your sexual dreams play an important role in understanding your sexual self. The symbolism of sexual dreams is varied, from images of exquisite eroticism that symbolize your most secret sexual fantasies to dark, dense images that swamp and suffocate you, symbolizing unresolved sexual fears and frustrations. They form a vast, creative tapestry for you to explore. Because of the huge creativity unleashed by the sleeping mind I feel that dream interpretation is made a more manageable process if we first identify three categories of sexual dream:

1. Overt sexual dreams
2. Veiled sexual dreams
3. Absurd sexual dreams.

All three types of dream provide equally valid (although obviously not the same) sources of insight into your subconscious desires, fears and frustrations.

Overt sexual dreams are those that seem to be based in reality. They may contain images of actual lovers, past or present, or simply yourself engaging in sexual activity. They are usually set in identifiable places that seem to make some sense, even if they are not places you would normally make love in; for example, a public park. The sexual activity is very definitely sexual and not camouflaged by the subconscious in any way. Essentially these dreams are quite believable. They do not necessarily have a happy ending. Some overtly sexual dreams may be distressing in some way; for example, containing images of being rejected by your lover (perhaps after you have argued in waking life). But they still seem to symbolize something that is possible and has an erotic basis.

Veiled sexual dreams, on the other hand, are sometimes at first hard to identify as sexual dreams. If you have a dream that seems interesting or has unusual imagery, how do you identify it as sexual? The key symbol that usually helps identify a veiled sexual dream is the recognition of sexual feelings of some sort within the dream images, or on waking from the dream. Taken at face value these images would not appear to relate to your sexual self. For example, you may find yourself dreaming of lying in a pit of writhing snakes. This might not at first seem like an obvious sexual image. In fact, it may seem on the surface to be a nightmarish one. However, you may be able to identify it as a sexual dream because the whole dream is somehow permeated with a sense of eroticism. Or you may wake feeling aroused or sexually frustrated, depending on the message your subconscious is trying to give you in this veiled or 'protected' manner.

Veiling sexual content, in the shape of obscured images, is one way that your subconscious can allow awareness of a particular issue or feeling to develop gradually in a non-threatening way. Of course, many people fail to notice this kind of subtle symbolism and consequently fail to develop an understanding of the particular issue or feeling at the heart of the message. You have to think through the dream images carefully to determine whether they contain any enlightening messages.

Absurd sexual dreams usually contain surprising images that in waking life the dreamer would never consciously think of as potentially sexually stimulating. For example, Elizabeth (*see page 112*) dreamed of having torrid sex with her boss who, in real life, she actively disliked. This to her was absolutely absurd. Elizabeth felt she would never ever consider her boss in a sexual light. And yet her subconscious cast them together in sexual activity.

Absurd dreams may also be about a fantastic wish fulfilment, for example, in which the dreamer has sex with a famous celebrity. In the dream the person enjoys this passionate sexual activity with someone who is out of their reach. On waking, most people wish their absurd dream could come true but realize it was simply their subconscious having some fun playing with sexual ideas that in real life would be impossible. Usually the dreamer has seen the celebrity that appears in their dream in a film or on television very recently.

NURTURING YOUR
SEXUAL SELF

A good starting point for interpreting, understanding and nurturing your sexual self and to gain a sense of what is going on in your deeper self is to look at your dreamscape. Dreamscapes are the dream backdrop; they form the general feeling of each dream. It can be anything your subconscious feels like painting for you. Imagine a dreamscape that consists of a raging sea of dark emotions. You are pitched through the dream before a backdrop of incredible intensity. Now consider a dreamscape in which a general sense of fulfilment permeates: you are aware of a tranquil, soothing, post-orgasmic sensation.

Another important step in nurturing your sexual self is to develop better recall of your sexual dreams and your dreams generally. Tuning into your inner self, and developing an awareness of the importance of dream symbolism, will help your recall of dreams. Generate a positive cycle: if you accept that dreams have an important role to play in gaining self-knowledge you will inevitably encourage an intuitive and open-minded attitude, which in turn will lead to better dream recall. This will lead to the appearance of more symbolic material to explore, then to a better understanding of your sexual self, and finally to the ability to look after your sexual self.

Finally, exploration of your sexual dreams will influence you as a whole person. By gaining awareness of your sexual self through analysis of your sexual dreams, you will develop an emotionally healthy outlook to sexual relationships that will in turn lead you to enjoy life more as a responsible, intuitive person comfortable with their sexuality. Understanding of your sexual dreams will enable you to reconcile difficult sexual feelings, which in the past have inhibited or frustrated you, and to improve your ability to communicate your needs to your lover and accommodate your lover's desires. As a result, you should achieve an enhanced sense of overall well-being as well as a more fulfilling sex life.

PART ONE

Practical Interpretation

Sexual dreams can arise from a surprising variety of sources, and it is sometimes difficult knowing where to start in their interpretation. They may relate to sexual activity you had the day before, a past sexual relationship, sexual longings you have for someone, or a deep-seated negative attitude or experience. Develop a positive approach to your dream analysis: unpleasant images or feelings may hold the key to releasing previously blocked or repressed emotions. Resolving such problems will lead to a more fulfilling emotional and sexual life – as well as more pleasurable sexual dreams.

This section shows you how to find the central dream symbol in a dream and how to use the 'DREAM' key to explore the possible meanings of your dream step by step. It offers advice on keeping a record of your dreams and provides techniques for shaping your dreams. The 'dreamercises' will enable you to tap into your conscious desires and enhance the sensual pleasure in your dreams. They are graded, each gradually increasing in their level of sensual content. Use them as you feel appropriate, building on your sexual confidence and enhancing your sense of well-being and contentment with your sexual self.

Exploring
Your Dreams

The key to successful dream interpretation is to remember that you 'own' your dream life. It is private to you and you need to allow yourself the freedom to experience it without fear and to explore it openly. Emotional openness is crucial when exploring your sexual dreams. It is important not to block out, or conceal, the true meaning of your dreams when you think about them in waking life. Many people do this without even being aware of what they are doing, and it is especially common with people who have struggled in the past with fear and anxiety over sexual issues.

In order to learn from your dreams you need to accept that they form part of your inner emotional self. Do not attempt to make a moral judgement about the content: there is no right or wrong about your dreams. When your dreams come to you, simply cherish the fact that you are gaining an insight into the 'secret garden' of your subconscious. And that is a special privilege. Sometimes the content may seem so sexually charged as to astound or shock you. If this is the case, remind yourself that everyone experiences dream content from time to time that surprises them – and they are very likely to keep it to themselves!

Your subconscious may be actively trying to conceal certain aspects of your sexual feelings. Alternatively, it may be gently propelling images into your sexual dreams that serve to make you think more deeply about your sexual self in a non-threatening way. Of course, the opposite may occur. Your subconscious may be so overwhelmed with deep-seated, negative feelings that it cannot contain them and when you are asleep, they tumble out in shocking or nightmarish form.

Remember, too, that your general level of well-being will have an effect on the nature and content of your dream life. If, for example, you are depressed or anxious about a current sexual relationship or a break-up you have recently experienced, your dream life is likely to be filled with negativity. You may find that you experience more nightmares than usual, perhaps about your ex-lover having sex with a phantom person (symbolizing your sense of loss over the sexual relationship). Or you may experience anxiety dreams based on unhappiness in your intimate relationship, in which sexual images take on nightmarish qualities.

In some ways you might prefer to avoid exploring such dreams but, in fact, learning to explore negative dreams, and taking the time to understand them, will enhance your self-knowledge. This, in turn, will enhance your emotional well-being, leading to dreams of a more uplifting nature.

DEVELOPING A POSITIVE MIND-SET

If you can overcome any emotional negativity about your sexual self and about the value of your dreams to your personal development, then you will be able to explore with an open mind the individual symbols that are woven into the rich tapestry of your dream life, and discover how they may guide you in your waking life. This positive, open and active exploration of your dreams will help you along the journey to discovering and developing your sexual self.

Acceptance that your dreams may contain crucial symbols of what is going on in your sexual self is important. Such conscious awareness and acceptance of the part dreams have to play in your life will allow your subconscious to reveal more freely feelings, attitudes and longings that have long been locked away. In this way your waking (conscious) decisions will impact on your subconscious emotional life.

A positive mind-set has been shown to facilitate all sorts of human activity. Research has shown that the outcomes of crucial employment situations, such as job interviews and business negotiations; sporting activities, such as competitive racing or games; and general mind and body performance and well-being are all improved by a positive mind-set. The achievement of positive results is due to a belief that you can cope with hurdles, that you will do your best, and that there will be positive benefits from simply trying something and learning from the experience. A positive mind-set is equally beneficial to attaining a greater understanding of your sexual self through the medium of your dreams.

As you become more accepting of your sexual self, more willing to develop your sexual relationships and more open to sexual communication with your lover, this will in turn enhance your dream life. Personal development often leads to more exaggerated or intense dream states and more frequent recollection of dreams. This is particularly true if previously you were nervous of potentially sexually charged content in your dreams. In effect, your dreaming potential increases as all levels of your consciousness become aware that you are developing as a sexual person.

SENSUAL EXERCISES

The sensual exercises that accompany many of the case studies contained within the Dream Finder (*see pages 40–135*) are designed to encourage your development as a person who positively enjoys their sexual relationships. I have created them so that they will guide you in the development of your sensuality and appreciation of the pleasures that an active sex life can bring. They allow you to explore your sensuality in a non-threatening way. These sensual exercises can provide the foundations for your future relationships – the way you approach lovers and allow them to share sexual intimacy with you.

Of course, what you practise within your sexual and romantic relationship during the day influences your dreamscapes at night. The sensual exercises that slowly develop throughout the book help you to gain an understanding of your sexual self; build your sexual self-confidence; allow you to heighten your sexual communication; and improve your understanding of your lover. These small steps will enhance your experiences in the 'secret garden' of your dream life.

A number of the sensual exercises will actually add generally to your personal development. This is because enhancing your ability to communicate with your lover will also give you the skills to communicate better in other areas. Also, as your confidence builds in your sensual self, your feelings about your whole self will be enhanced. Our sexuality is such an integral part of how we define ourselves as people that by enhancing one we cannot help but affect the other positively!

I have also created four 'dreamercises', which are described at the end of this section (*see pages 32–5*). By carrying out any one of these dreamercises before falling asleep, you should be able to increase the sensual content of any subsequent dreams you experience. Not only will this give you pleasure, but it will also help you to develop your sensuality in waking life, thereby increasing your sexual self-confidence.

RECORDING YOUR DREAMS

Developing a readiness to interpret your dreams means that you must take simple practical steps to enable you to record your dreams. Ensure that you have a torch or nightlight by your bed, so that you can record any dream you have if you wake during the night. Keep a pen and notepad ready and write down the basic dream theme together with feelings and details you can recall before going back to sleep.

If you sleep right through the night to wake in the morning, before you do anything else, relax and clear your head to allow any dreams to come floating back to you. Consciously prevent any thoughts about the coming day from interrupting this process, while you free your mind for the purpose of recollection. You will find that taking these few moments benefits your well-being generally as you will start the day feeling relaxed.

You might like to begin a dream diary in which you enter the notes you have jotted down from the moment of waking. As you look back over this diary, you may find a pattern taking shape in your dreams that is reflected in your waking relationships. They may even seem to predict what is going to happen. For example, if in one particular dream you take a step forward in your lovemaking, you will then find that you actually take a step forward with your lover in your sexual relationship. Your subconscious is usually a couple of steps ahead of your conscious thoughts.

Using the 'dream' key

Even the most intuitive people wonder where they should start in exploring the meaning of their dreams. This is particularly true of sexual dreams. These may contain dramatic or graphic images as well as more subtle feelings, which go straight to the core of your being. Many people find such potentially elaborate or complex images confusing, and are unsure of how to separate out the various images and feelings.

I believe a practical, step-by-step approach is the most helpful way to begin. To help you along the journey of developing your dream awareness I have devised the following DREAM key to give you a framework for analysing your dreams. Using it should heighten your understanding of your sexual dreams and ensure that you do not miss anything that may cast light on your sexual self or relationship. Even once you become more in tune with the wonderful world of your dream life you may still wish to use this simple key.

Consider the word 'DREAM' as an acronym with each letter representing the following individual words:

DETAIL

RECOGNITION

EMOTIONS

ACTION

MEANING

Each of these words indicates an area to explore in any particular dream. Work through each area in turn to build up a complete picture and uncover the hidden meaning of your dream.

DETAIL: What details stand out in your dream recollection? Is it a dream bursting with intricacies or are there only one or two details or images that you can recall?

RECOGNITION: Did you recognize any of the people, places or even feelings in your dream? Or was your dreamscape completely unfamiliar and were the people (if any) unknown to you?

EMOTIONS: During the course of your dream what was the overriding emotional experience you had? For example, was the predominant feeling one of sexual arousal, satisfaction, frustration or anxiety?

ACTION: There is activity in all dreams, even if it is only subtle. What is important is the role you take in this activity. Did you take a passive role, in which everything was done to you, or you watched everything take place? Or did you take an active role, in which you led the dream activity, or did things to others?

MEANING: At an intuitive level, what do your basic instincts tell you about the meaning of your dream? Your initial intuitive interpretation may well help you to build up a fuller picture. You may start out with an initial belief that your dream is telling you, for example, that you are sexually dissatisfied. Then, with further exploration, you may come to develop a fuller picture, concluding that you are not satisfied because you will not let go when you are with your lover.

When you have explored each area, link them together to help you paint the most complete picture of the substance and meaning inherent in your dream.

FINDING THE KEY DREAM SYMBOL

Most dreams contain a key symbol even if, at first, they seem to be a blur of indecipherable feelings or images. The key dream symbol is the one that reveals the deeper, subconscious activity of your mind. It is pivotal to unlocking a deeper meaning within a dream. Of course, many dream symbols simply paint a picture like a story and you can read them quite easily. These may or may not contain enlightening meanings. And you must bear in mind that not all dreams contain revelations. Sometimes they have quite simply linked together recent events in a playful manner, without necessarily casting light on your deeper feelings.

To discover a key dream symbol first analyse any unexpected twists and turns in your dream as these are the places where your subconscious has decided either to 'protect' you from a threatening dream path or to throw something up for you to consider. Next, if one dream image is particularly vivid, strong or emotion-filled, explore it more carefully. With practice you will come to find that you can quickly identify the key dream symbol in your dreams. In addition, as you become more aware of your sexual self and in tune with your sexual relationships, you will become more adept at plucking out the key dream symbol from your sexual dreams.

Shaping Your Dreams

Now that you understand the essential principles of interpretation it is time to learn how to shape your sexual dreams. I have devised a series of 'dreamercises' (dream exercises) to help you guide and intensify your dream experiences. Just as people use techniques, such as visualization, during their waking life to influence their feelings and behaviour, so dreamercises influence your dreams while you are asleep. As you learn to relax into them and allow your mind to let go of past dream images they will help you to enjoy the new images your subconscious creates in your dream life. Remember, everything about our nature is interactive.

Just as feelings locked in our subconscious can influence our dreamscapes (and waking behaviour!), so our waking thoughts and actions can influence the way we dream. Once you have learned that you can have some influence over your dreamscapes your confidence in your sexual self will increase.

I have included four dreamercises here to help you to develop a new sensuality in your dreams. All four dreamercises should be practised just before you fall asleep when you are feeling relaxed. If you catch yourself thinking about something sensual during the day you may want to make a mental note to include those thoughts in any of the following dreamercises.

DREAMERCISE ONE
Sensual You

This first dreamercise seeks to enhance your dreams at the most basic but important level – your sexual self. It is particularly good for people who feel out of touch with their sexual self.

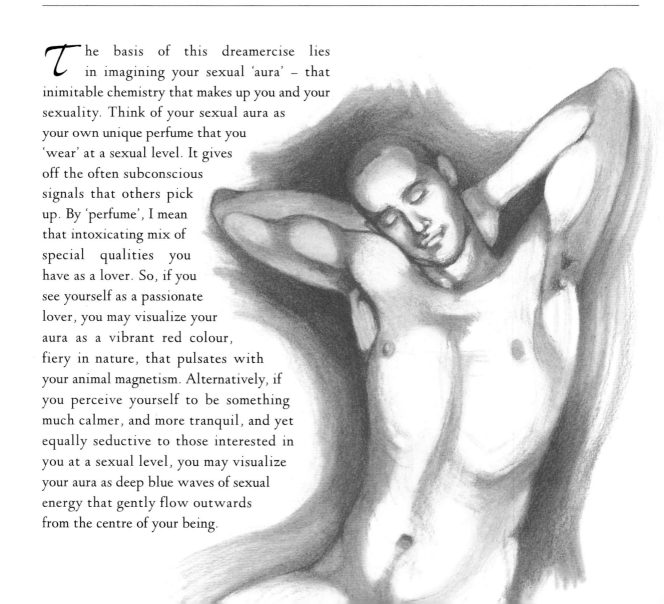

The basis of this dreamercise lies in imagining your sexual 'aura' – that inimitable chemistry that makes up you and your sexuality. Think of your sexual aura as your own unique perfume that you 'wear' at a sexual level. It gives off the often subconscious signals that others pick up. By 'perfume', I mean that intoxicating mix of special qualities you have as a lover. So, if you see yourself as a passionate lover, you may visualize your aura as a vibrant red colour, fiery in nature, that pulsates with your animal magnetism. Alternatively, if you perceive yourself to be something much calmer, and more tranquil, and yet equally seductive to those interested in you at a sexual level, you may visualize your aura as deep blue waves of sexual energy that gently flow outwards from the centre of your being.

WHAT YOU DO

When you feel relaxed and ready for sleep, conjure up your vision of your sexual aura. Begin by considering all the qualities you possess as a lover and all those you could potentially possess. Give your aura shape and substance through your imagination. Feel the pleasure others might sense in you. Be really positive about yourself – this is no time for modesty. Allow your mind to wander over these pleasurable images with a wonderful sexual aura that excites you and others. Now consider the deep sleep you will experience. Allow your mind to let go of everything but thoughts of your sexual aura. This moment of tranquillity and enjoyment will help shape sensual dreams for your pleasure.

DREAMERCISE TWO

Sensual Beginnings

What is your fantasy seduction? Everyone daydreams about how they might seduce a person they are attracted to, or what they would do if they ran into their favourite film or pop star. It is part of human nature to take a break from the more mundane aspects of life and daydream about fantasy scenarios.

This dreamercise is all about taking your fantasy of that first moment of seduction and using it to shape a glorious sexual dream. It is particularly good for people who have inhibited sexual attitudes as it allows you to be more courageous without risking anything.

WHAT YOU DO

When relaxed and about to fall asleep, clear your mind of all the random thoughts that may compete for your attention. Throw your mind open to a scene of seduction that arouses you. Choose the fantasy scenario that works for you.

Do you entrance a new lover with breathtaking seduction? Or do you surprise an old lover with new-found sensual knowledge? Shape the beginning of a sexual dream and then allow your subconscious to go into sensual freefall and create the rest of the dream unfettered by any negative images.

When you are successful in setting in motion such a chain of subconscious dream image connections, it can lead to fascinating results, providing you with real insight into where your subconscious would like to lead you unhindered by conscious barriers. Learn from this!

DREAMERCISE THREE
Sensual Pathways

Once you have successfully carried out the sensual you and sensual beginnings dreamercises, you will have become more at ease with your sexual self and will be ready to develop your sexuality. You are now ready to try the sensual pathways dreamercise, which requires a sexually confident and open mind-set. This dreamercise is the vehicle for creating a fuller sexual dreamscape.

This dreamercise involves thinking through your favourite fantasy, from sensual beginnings to erotic meetings, by following an imaginary sensual pathway to see where your mind leads you. Indulging in your sensual pathway allows you to enjoy your sensual self in a private way that will enhance your feelings of sensuality.

WHAT YOU DO

Begin by freeing your thoughts just as you are about to fall asleep. Now visualize yourself in a lush garden. Allow yourself to visualize all sorts of exotic tropical flowers and lush plants. Who might you find amongst this beautiful scenery? What would they be doing? Your fantasy lover might be waiting just for you. Or a lover past or present may be lounging there, basking in warm sunlight.

You are feeling wonderful and confident, ready to try anything you have ever imagined.

Build up an entire journey through your secret garden punctuated by erotic images from your own secret world of desire. Allow yourself to stop and enjoy the moment at each point in your sensual pathway. Do not rush down the path. Consider carefully each erotic event that takes place along your pathway. The erotic 'punctuations' that you meditate upon in this way before you fall asleep will help shape your dreams to come. For as you drift off into sleep your mind will continue to follow the erotic images of your pathway, developing new subconscious encounters that will prove enlightening on waking.

Keep a notepad by your bed. Then, when you wake – either during the night or the next morning – note down anything you can remember of your dreamscapes and the feelings you have about the sensual experiences. Analyse your dream using the DREAM key (*see pages 29–30*) to discover its inherent meaning.

DREAMERCISE FOUR
The Final Climax

You are feeling more and more confident about exploring your sexuality,
which is a very positive development! Now you would like your sexual dreams
to conclude with a wonderful, all-encompassing orgasmic sensation. This
dreamercise allows you to create the sexual ending that will satisfy you.
No longer will you be left feeling frustrated in your dreams.

The final climax dreamercise is very flexible, allowing you to choose how you will shape the climax in your dreams. You may, for example, take a sexual dream you can recall from the past and give it the climax you would like. Where that dream left you feeling dissatisfied you may now create a satisfying ending. Or you may prefer to create a sensual pathway with the satisfying ending you want.

WHAT YOU DO
As you relax, preparing for sleep, think about the most wonderful orgasm you have ever had (it may be one you had on your own). Can you recall it in delicious detail? Is this how you would like your next erotic dream to end – with complete satisfaction? Perhaps you have never experienced an earth-shattering orgasm and you would like to dream of one. It is time to connect with this wonderful reality or your ultimate fantasy of what such an orgasm would be like.

As you progress along the path you would like your dreaming to take, approach the final climax with intimate detail. For example, you may place your present lover firmly in your dreamercise images. They are pleasuring you by teasing you in every conceivable way. First they gently bind your wrists and ankles so that you have to give yourself up to them completely. Next they gently sweep sensual oils all over your body, taking time over your most erogenous and intimate zones. Then they use their lips and tongue to bring you nearer your climax, running these the length of your body and circling your most sensitive areas. But they do not quite let you reach orgasm.

Now imagine the final orgasmic release you would like to experience, limbs thrashing, crying out for more, gasping with pleasure. Relaxing into sleep with this final sensual image in your mind will help to shape erotic dreams that will fulfil you sexually.

PART TWO

Dream Finder

*T*his section contains twenty-four dreams recounted to me by men and women that highlight a wide range of sexual issues. Each dream case study is illustrated and contains practical interpretation, dream analysis and suggestions for resolving the issues revealed by the dream. Accompanying many of the dream case studies are questionnaires and related themes to help you in the interpretation of your own dreams. In many cases specific sensual exercises are suggested, which were actually carried out by the dreamer concerned.

The dreams in this section cover a wide variety of sexual topics and are grouped according to type of dream. There are eight overtly sexual dreams, in which the imagery is clearly sexual (*see pages 40–71*); ten veiled sexual dreams, in which the subconscious has protected the dreamer by disguising the sexual content (*see pages 72–111*); and six absurd sexual dreams, in which the content of the dreams is sexual but seems ridiculous to the dreamer (*see pages 112–35*).

You may find it helpful to familiarize yourself with the three categories of dream by reading through all the case studies before beginning to interpret your own dreams. Alternatively, you may prefer to select the dream case study that most closely resembles your own recent dream by looking at the theme descriptions detailed overleaf.

Dream Case Studies

When you recall a dream that you are not sure how to interpret, the first step to take is to decide to which of the three dream categories it belongs: is it an overtly sexual dream, a veiled sexual dream or an absurd sexual dream? You may then want to read through all the dreams in that section, together with their analysis, to determine whether any of the sexual issues raised by those dreams seem relevant to your attitudes or situation. Even if they do not, you will undoubtedly find the analysis of the dreams helpful when analysing your own. Perhaps an issue of sexuality raised in relation to a dream from one of the other two categories actually relates more closely to your feelings and life.

You may find that one of the dreams in the Dream Finder is similar in theme to your own. To help you identify the dream case study that most closely resembles your own, the theme of each dream is summarized here. For example, perhaps in your dream you were surrounded by dirt or mud and the images were overtly sexual. This is similar in theme to Mary's dream (*see page 92*). Consequently, by studying Mary's dream and its interpretation, you will gain insights into the symbolism and overall meaning of your own dream, and will find helpful pointers on

resolving the issues concerned by reading that part of the analysis.

Where your dream images do not appear to match any particular case study, but one of the dreams strikes a chord with you, careful study of the analysis of that dream and situation of that dreamer may help you to understand your own sexual behaviour and feelings better. Questionnaires are also listed, so you can turn directly to one that seems of immediate relevance, even if the subject of the dream it accompanies does not appear to be the same.

Longing for Intimacy

"My lover was passionately performing oral sex as if I were his banquet.
He feasted for an eternity. The pleasure was intense and continued to mount
higher and higher until I felt I would burst ... but I never climaxed.
On waking, my heart was pounding.
I felt anxious and vulnerable, as if
my soul had been bared."

Background and Interpretation

Jane has difficulty with intimacy, at both an emotional and sexual level. This stems from some childhood unhappiness that she experienced. Her present relationship with Peter is causing her a great deal of anguish, and Jane has finally opened up to discuss the problems with her lover. His reaction was mixed: in part he felt empathy for Jane's suffering, but he also felt bewildered about how he should approach her in a way that would not cause her distress. However, Jane sees her new-found openness as positive progress, even if the effect it has had seems to be adding to her problems right now. Their sexual relationship is still unsatisfactory.

ANALYSING JANE'S DREAM

The dream imagery combined with waking life experiences reveal the meaning of this dream. Jane's dream demonstrates her passion for her lover behind her fragile façade. Her conscious awareness that the sexual intimacy in her current relationship is being blocked by past unhappiness is reflected by what happens in her dream. The intense arousal that she experiences represents her sexual needs. Allowing her lover to perform oral sex – one of the most intimate sexual techniques – shows that Jane really desires true intimacy.

Oral sex as a theme is quite common in the dreams of those who have problems with intimacy. The subconscious throws images of oral sex forward as a kind of internal challenge. It is forcing the dreamer to acknowledge the intimacy they are missing with powerful images that strike right to the heart. Jane's inability to 'let go' and reach orgasm in the dream reveals that she is still chained to her painful past and needs to work on this before she will be able to let go and climax in her waking life.

RESOLVING THE ISSUES

In addition to continuing her counselling, Jane tried the following two sensual exercises that help to reduce the fear of intimacy.

Trust building

Each partner writes down one sexual activity they have been frightened to try with the other – or even, perhaps, at any point in their life. They exchange notes. Together they open the notes and then try each activity. These sexual activities can be as simple or as complex as you like, from 'I'd like to expose my breasts to my lover' to 'I'd like to choose a sexual position to try'. They can even be very specific about a time and place to make love in a particular way.

Advanced trust building

Both partners agree on an erogenous zone to be explored on the partner who has a fear of intimacy. That person is then blindfolded and allows their lover to gently caress the selected zone on the understanding that they can stop the exercise at any time they wish. The idea is to learn to relax and enjoy the sensation, and give themselves up to their partner's touch.

Assess Your Sexual Intimacy

If you think you may be experiencing problems in becoming truly intimate with your partner, try answering the following five questions. Each question has three optional answers. Score three points for each answer a); score two points for each answer b); and score one point for each answer c).

1 *Are you honest with your partner about your ability/ inability to achieve orgasm?*
   a) Yes
   b) Most of the time
   c) No

2 *Do you feel a sense of unease or anxiety when your partner makes sexual overtures?*
   a) Never
   b) Sometimes
   c) Frequently

3 *Do you fear rejection by your partner if you turn down their sexual advances?*
   a) Never
   b) Sometimes
   c) Frequently

4 *Do you feel free and able to describe what arouses you to your partner?*
   a) Yes
   b) Sometimes
   c) Never, although I'd like to

5 *If you experience discomfort of any kind in lovemaking would you tell your partner?*
   a) Yes
   b) It depends on the circumstances
   c) No, although I'd want to

Score 11 to 15:
HIGH LEVEL OF SEXUAL INTIMACY
You experience a high level of sexual intimacy with your partner. Your emotional awareness enables you to communicate your sexual needs at an intimate level. Allow your dreams to guide you to more creative ways of expressing your sexual needs. Try the unusual positions they may contain, and recreate the depth of feeling in your real lovemaking.

Score 6 to 10:
MODERATE LEVEL OF SEXUAL INTIMACY
Sometimes you do not feel secure enough to communicate your needs openly. In interpreting your sexual dreams look for symbols that express your subconscious desire to gain more intimacy. Feelings of longing in dreams may be particularly important. What are you longing for? Is it to touch your lover more intimately? Is it to call out to them? Touching in your dream implies that you wish to be more physically expressive. Calling out signals the fear that you are not expressing yourself. Explore dream symbols that indicate a fear of intimacy, such as:
• the lover that comes back and forth to your bed
• changing lovemaking positions before you are ready
• disruptions to lovemaking, such as a pet leaping on to the bed or the bed disappearing.
Re-examine your questionnaire answers, taking particular note of any in which you scored one or two points. These are the difficult areas for you.

Score 1 to 5:

Low Level of Sexual Intimacy

You may allow lovers to dominate your sex life, or do not have the courage to express your needs. You may seek lovers who are self-centred as subconsciously you know they will not make demands for real intimacy. Analyse sexual dreams. Do you feel anxious, fearful or out of control with overtly sexual content? Do you run from, or feel overwhelmed by, sexual themes in your dreams? On waking, do you feel sick with worry? Other symbolism to be aware of is:

- your lover is faceless
- you are blind in your dream, although you, as a dreamer, can 'see' yourself
- your lover is on top of you and you feel smothered
- your lover is behind you and you cannot see them
- you are unable to reach orgasm, as in Jane's dream
- the dream moves quickly from pleasure to nightmare.

These all suggest your subconscious is communicating to you. Explore where this fear of sexual intimacy originates. Then communicate your fears to your lover, to jointly achieve a satisfying sex life together.

Related Themes

Licking/sucking

Usually these oral activities signify enjoyment in the present sexual relationship. Tenderness in these activities symbolizes deeper feelings of love. Eagerness in these actions symbolizes the earthiness of the dreamer's feelings. When combined with anxiety, fear or unhappiness, these actions suggest coercion in the sexual relationship. You feel that you have to do things to please your partner.

Gentle nibbles

This action signifies an inhibition about fully engaging in your sexual relationship. You cannot quite relax and enjoy erotic love.

Closed lips/refusal to allow anything to pass

You wish to prevent a sexual encounter. Your subconscious may be telling you that you are not ready to make love with a new partner. Alternatively, the balance in your relationship has changed and you are closing down sexually.

Inability to swallow/choking sensation

You feel overwhelmed by either the sexual demands being made on you or your own sexual impulses. You are unable to 'stomach' what is happening, so your subconscious does not allow your oral reflexes to work.

Being force-fed

Such a strong image symbolizes repugnance towards some aspect of your sex life. Usually force-feeding relates to a dread, or fear, of oral sex. But it can also symbolize a fear of sex generally.

Overriding Sexual Demands

"At first I was standing over my partner, Ron, wearing only a skimpy thong. We were on a bed that was soft and bouncy. I was laughing and jumping up and down with my breasts bouncing freely. I felt fantastic and excited. I shouted, 'Bounce with me!' over and over again. Then I noticed that Ron was looking odd. He seemed to be saying something but I couldn't hear him. I started to get angry, although I still wanted to make love to him. I lay on top of him with my legs straddling his, rubbing my breasts against his chest. I started demanding: 'Come on, get inside of me!' I was feeling so frustrated. Yet for some reason he couldn't respond. He was sinking deeper into the folds of the bed – I thought the covers were swallowing him up."

Background and Interpretation

Sandra and Ron had been together for eighteen months. They had developed a strong emotional bond but their sexual relationship was on shaky grounds. Sandra had high expectations in the bedroom and they argued over her sexual demands. It was not that Ron did not enjoy sex – he did – but Sandra had always adored sex. She liked to have sex frequently and was not averse to spelling out exactly what she wanted in the bedroom, sitting room or wherever the mood took her. Her voracious sexual appetite had caused problems in several of her previous relationships. Some men had found her demands intimidating, and had broken things off with Sandra because of this. She had not worried about the matter before but now her dream concerned her. It was so vivid and seemed to contain a message.

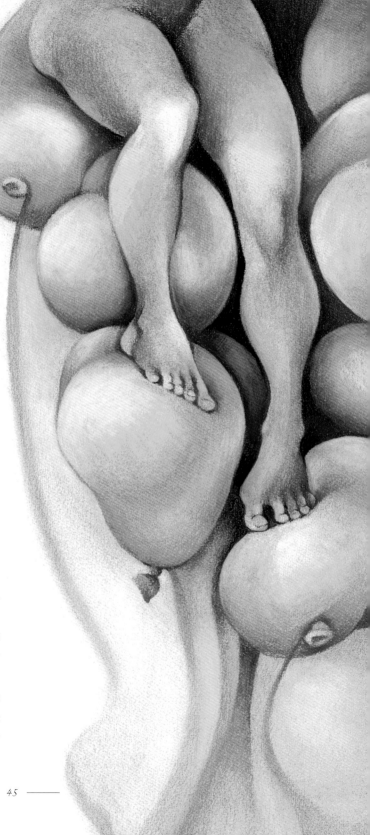

ANALYSING SANDRA'S DREAM

Sandra's dream clearly reflects the demanding sexual role she plays in waking life. At the beginning of the dream she is standing above Ron, symbolizing her position of control in their sexual relationship. Bouncing on the bed with a sense of sensual enjoyment indicates her outright enjoyment of sex, and shouting at him to join her reveals how keen she is for him to come along for the ride with her!

Sandra's position of control does not lead to satisfaction, and tension develops in the dream. Ron is trying to speak but Sandra cannot hear him: this is her unconscious telling her, 'you're not listening to him'. She is angry but still wants to make love, straddling Ron and demanding he enters her. Her dominating position and incessant demands go unnoticed by Ron, who appears to be becoming enveloped by the bed. Her subconscious is trying to tell her that this is not the way to engage Ron sexually. The bed symbolizes Sandra at a sexual level: the enveloping folds represent the depths of her vagina. She is quite literally swallowing Ron up with her demands.

The dream is telling Sandra that her strength of character is a weakness in the bedroom, leading her to ignore Ron at a sexual level. She does not notice whether he is even aroused or whether he even wants sex every time she does. Her anger at not having her demands met and his frustration at feeling he must continually meet her demands whether he likes it or not may eventually threaten the whole relationship.

RESOLVING THE ISSUES

At twenty-eight Sandra knew it was time to sort out her approach to sex. Of course she had been aware in the past that some of her lovers were unhappy with her sexual style. They had told her as much when they finished the relationship with her. But until her relationship with Ron, she had responded rather stubbornly, maintaining that her approach to sex was part of her nature, and why should she change her nature for her lover? Her attitude was rather arrogant as a sexual relationship needs to encompass both partners' approaches.

Looking back over her life, Sandra pinpointed how deeply her strong mother had influenced her. Sandra admired her mother, who had forged a successful career after divorcing Sandra's father. Sandra had learned at a young age that it was important to look after herself, and she went on to enjoy a successful career too. What she now needed to understand was that her rather forceful approach to life was not always appropriate to the situation. In particular she realized that she was going to have to soften her seduction techniques with Ron if she wanted the relationship to succeed.

Sensual Exercises

There are a number of sensual exercises designed to soften a sexually demanding nature in cases where it is having a negative effect on lovers. Of course, if you are in a relationship with someone who enjoys your demanding approach – who wants to be moulded by you – there is no need to change your approach. You may still like to try these exercises to increase your flexibility in your sexual relationships.

Listen and learn

This is probably the most important step you can take in toning down your demanding sexual style. Take a step back from leading in making love by speaking less and listening more to your lover. Listen to what they say and pay attention to all of their lovemaking noises. Their sighs, moans and crying out will give you a lot of intimate information about their enjoyment.

Taking turns

Sexually demanding people tend to be the initiators of sexual encounters. This does not allow a 'quieter' lover to learn more about their own powers of initiation. They simply take a back seat and the spontaneity may be lost from the relationship. Encourage your lover to initiate sex on a more regular basis. Tell them that you will not approach them – that it's their turn next time they are in the mood for love to let you know. Be patient and show them you mean what you say by giving them time.

Soften your tone

People are very often unaware of how much their tone of voice conveys in terms of lovemaking. Even if you have altered your physical approach to show more awareness of your lover's needs, your tone of voice may still need to be softened. Practise saying

Related Themes

Images that take over someone in sexual dreams are quite common. They can, as in Sandra's dream, symbolize the dreamer's own sexual power but more frequently they represent a lack of power within a sexual relationship. The context of the dream will reveal which way around it is in your life.

Being swamped by your lover

A dream image where your lover swamps, engulfs or even swallows you, clearly symbolizes your lack of power in the sexual relationship. Try the sensual exercises that Henry tried on page 110.

Being swallowed by an animal

This can symbolize a need for emotional protection – a longing to be swallowed up whole and kept safe. It reflects deep-rooted

fears concerning sex – that it is frightening or threatening at some level.

Being engulfed in flames, or flame-like images

Sex is quite literally getting too hot. Where once you were content in a sexual relationship, now you are unhappy. Flames in sexual dreams suggest a need for immediate action – the relationship is heading for a crisis.

Being engulfed by a pit

This symbolizes that your lover is actively trying to take over your sexual life, or even your whole relationship. It is similar in form to Sandra's dream image of the bedclothes engulfing Ron. Tumbling or falling into a pit indicates that you are giving up control as you become more passive.

something seductive in private by yourself, using a range of different tones. Notice the differences in effect each has on you. Then, the next time you make love, try whispering seductively in the tone you now feel confident is not demanding. Gently tell your partner about your enjoyment.

Sensual beginnings dreamercise

Sandra used this dreamercise (*see page 33*) in an unusual way. She explored fantasy scenarios in which she was the one being seduced rather than the other way around in order to encourage dreams in which she derived pleasure in being led by Ron.

Concerns
About Sexuality

"I was in a very dark, yet warm, place. A steamy mist was swirling around me. I felt excited and terrified in equal measure. The mist seemed to guide me to the ground, which was hot and moist. I was lolling about and enjoying the earthiness of touching my own body. Next I was aware of wonderful hands caressing me. They seemed to touch me in the most fabulous way. Then the person took shape and kissed me. It was a woman, which didn't trouble me in the dream even though I've never had a sexual encounter with a woman in waking life. In fact, I felt excited as she had the softest lips and I drew them to mine passionately. I never wanted the kiss to end. We stroked each other's bodies passionately for what seemed like an eternity. Then suddenly I was aware of an awkwardness and asked her if she had any clothes for me to put on. My dream ended abruptly."

Background and Interpretation

Angela was having a casual relationship with Mark. It was not very satisfying sexually but they had a good laugh together. Angela's past sexual relationships had varied from the mundane to the wildly experimental.

Angela had never slept with a woman and although she occasionally fantasized about a 'threesome' containing a woman, she had never had a lesbian sex dream. It made her extremely uncomfortable. She could not shake the thought out of her head: 'Could I have lesbian or bisexual leanings?'

The thought made her anxious. Angela's mind raced forwards in time, bringing with it more uncomfortable thoughts: 'If I do have a relationship with a woman, do I tell anyone? My parents would die if I brought home a woman. Should I tell Mark about my dream and worries?' Angela was falling victim to many of the anxieties people have when they think their sexuality may step outside the norm. Many people experience intense feelings for both sexes at different points in their life. Sexuality is far more fluid than many realize. When you desire someone it is better to think of them as an individual rather than as a representative of their sex. Would they be a good partner and lover? Angela could not stop herself from categorizing her sexuality. (Was she 'straight', 'lesbian' or 'bisexual'?) She began actively to embrace this potentially damaging way of thinking.

ANALYSING ANGELA'S DREAM

The darkness of Angela's dreamscape symbolizes her doubts (a sunny, bright dreamscape would have symbolized the opposite). They cast a shadow over all the events. The mist is suggestive of femininity, her subconscious throwing up a gentle swirling sensation. The stage is set for a feminine encounter. The hot, moist ground indicates the earthiness of her sensuality

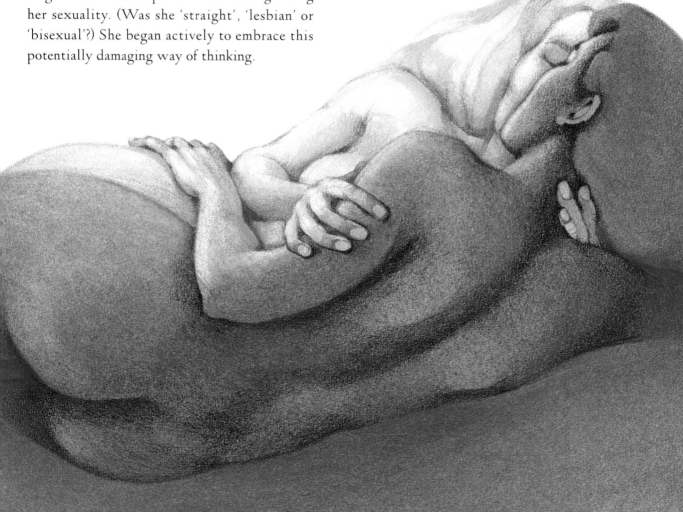

– Angela has been very experimental in the past. All these elements come together to suggest diversity in her sexual feelings.

The sexual charge in the dream initially comes from her but then another woman joins her. The sensual hands arrive first as if to 'break the news' slowly to Angela that it is a woman who is pleasuring her. Her subconscious allows the sexual chemistry between her and the woman to unfold step by step. Angela is accepting at first, even taking the lead by drawing the woman's lips to hers. And she thoroughly enjoys the kissing and touching that takes place. The abrupt stop to this pleasurable encounter is caused by Angela's defence mechanisms breaking through. By asking for clothes she 'protects' herself from reaching a final climax, which would be a sign of acceptance of enjoyment of lesbian sex.

RESOLVING THE ISSUES

With exploration, Angela came to accept that she was attracted to women and men. This was something she had chosen to put to the back of her mind. She recalled an intense, secret passion she had had for a roommate at college. She had regularly fantasized about her in the relative 'safety' of a threesome with her then boyfriend. After careful consideration, Angela decided not to share her feelings with Mark as she did not see the relationship developing. In fact, she envisaged a time when they would be simply friends. At that point she thought she might open up to him about her fluid sexuality.

Angela felt far less emotional tension in her life as she came to accept that one day she might have a sexual relationship with another woman. She practised a number of sensual exercises that helped her reach self-acceptance.

Sensual Exercises

Acceptance of your whole sexual self will enhance your emotional well-being. You may like to try these exercises whether or not you have concerns about your sexual orientation.

Nurturing visualization

Take a few quiet moments for yourself and close your eyes. Think of your unique sensuality: I call this your sensual essence. Visualize your sensual essence as a beautiful thing. It can take any form you like as long as it represents whatever your sensuality means to you. For example, you may choose a sleek,

glossy animal or a beautiful flower. In the visualization feel the beauty of your sensual essence. Care, respect and love it. This makes you a special person in terms of your sensuality.

Sensual acceptance

Make a full list of all the aspects of yourself that you feel are sensual. Be thorough. Include everything from the feel of your hair to the softness of your inner thighs and the way you kiss. Describe each aspect in intimate detail. Accept your sensual self. If you are in a partnership right now, then take the time to describe each other in this way. It will make you both feel wonderful to know that the other has identified so much sensuality within you.

Your sexual rights

Think through and write down a self-affirmation about your sexual rights. This is about your right, as an adult, to enjoy fulfilling sexual relationships with the person or people of your choice. Keep this with you and whenever you doubt your sexual right, re-read it and believe it. Allow no one to take this sense of yourself away from you. You have only one life and you may live it loving any other consenting adult you choose.

Related Themes

Sunny, bright dreamscape

Such a dreamscape indicates happiness within your sexual relationship. It may also, depending on the context, symbolize a readiness to become more creative with your lover. Any sexual images that take place in a sunny dreamscape are likely to be pleasurable.

Raining

If sexual images take place in a rainy dreamscape it symbolizes unhappiness or even a depressed attitude towards some kind of sexual activity. Being soaked by rain indicates vulnerability – you cannot control what is happening sexually in your life at the moment.

Thunder

Dark, thunder-filled dreamscapes symbolize deeply rooted sexual fears. Images contained in these dreamscapes are usually laced with anxiety or have nightmarish qualities. Cracking of thunder may also symbolize a sexually submissive nature. You are prepared to go 'under the whip', although at another level you may actually like to prevent your submissive side from showing.

Foggy/cloudy

This sort of dreamscape, in which sexual activities are partly obscured by fog or low-lying clouds, suggests that you are hiding your true sexual feelings from yourself and others. Your subconscious is providing a shroud for certain images partly to conceal their meaning. Perhaps you are not quite ready to face up to your true sexual desires or some problems you are experiencing in your sexual relationship.

Shimmering

You are ready for sexual exploration. The shimmering signifies positive sexual tension and a desire to explore new erotic territory. Enjoy this time of adventure.

Loss of Erection

"I keep having the same dream. It always starts the same. I'm alone in a bedroom that's more like a hotel room than my own bedroom. It has some familiar features, like the bed I'm lying on is my bed. And familiar clothes are strewn around. I try to clutch at them from my position on the bed but I can't scoop them up. I'm naked and I start playing with my erect penis. It feels good as I stroke myself but then the telephone rings, distracting me. I don't know the person at the other end but I sense that they know what I'm doing. I feel angry while we speak. I notice the pleasurable sensations leave my body and my penis starts to shrink. I'm getting more and more nervous talking to them. It sometimes ends there and I awake feeling upset and uncomfortable. Other times I keep speaking to the person on the phone and try to push out of my mind the thoughts of my limp penis. I actually feel worse when it ends this way – there's a feeling of guilt for some odd reason."

Background and Interpretation

Jeremy had been living with Cassie for six months. Prior to moving in together they had dated on and off for two years. At twenty-six Jeremy felt too young to commit to marriage, and, in fact, he had only agreed to share a flat with Cassie when she had threatened to end their relationship if he did not. She wanted to see him make some form of commitment even if he still would not talk about marriage. At about the same time that they had moved in together Jeremy had come under pressure at work to meet more difficult targets.

For the last five months he had experienced loss of erection most of the times he made love with Cassie. It was occurring more frequently as time went by, and Jeremy was feeling panicky. He wondered if this was the end of sex as he had always enjoyed it. 'What was happening to him?' Jeremy was now finding excuses to go to bed later than Cassie and she felt a void was growing between them. Every time she brought up the subject of their lovemaking, Jeremy became very uncomfortable and tried to end or change the conversation. He had not told Cassie that when he masturbates in the shower he can maintain his erection.

ANALYSING JEREMY'S DREAM
Jeremy's recurring dream meant that he could not escape his erection difficulties.

The problem was there, during waking life, when trying to make love with Cassie, and when he would like to have some peace of mind – during sleep. The dream itself, while reflecting his worries, also illuminated his deeper, subconscious feelings about his relationship as a whole with Cassie.

Finding himself in a room that only partly resembles their room symbolizes his ambivalence about sharing a flat with Cassie. The familiar aspects of the room indicate that in some ways he feels comfortable with it, while the parts that resemble a featureless hotel room – a dispassionate place that lacks comfort – indicate that in some ways he does not. That his clothes are strewn around the room represents the carefree 'bachelor' life his subconscious craves. When he fails to scoop them up he reveals his feeling of disappointment at not holding on to this freedom.

Playing with his penis while totally naked symbolizes how exposed Jeremy feels. His subconscious allows him to slip back to the old pleasures of enjoying his erect penis. This is interrupted by the stranger on the telephone. Jeremy's unconscious allows this protective mechanism – talking to a person on the phone is less threatening than talking to someone in the same room. The phone allays only some of his concerns, however: his penis starts to shrink, reflecting his loss of erection during waking life. He feels anger at the loss of pleasure due to the 'interruption' by another person, symbolic of Cassie's interruption of his sexual enjoyment. The two endings to his dream represent his conversations in waking life with Cassie. When they end abruptly he feels upset and uncomfortable, similar to the general discomfort he feels while awake. The second ending, where he keeps talking to the person while pushing away thoughts of his shrinking penis, reflects how he feels when Cassie has tried to talk to him – guilty, because he won't talk to her at an honest level. And guilty about successfully masturbating – he can maintain an erection on his own.

RESOLVING THE ISSUES

There is a battle within Jeremy about what he really wants from a relationship at this point. His dream helps to clarify that by forcing him to be more honest with Cassie. Jeremy decided to come clean with Cassie about his negative feelings. Telling her he was not ready to consider marriage was a risk as she might choose to leave, but he realized he must have the courage to face this. It was not fair to Cassie to string her along with only a half-hearted commitment.

After clearing the air, with tears on both sides, Cassie said she would be happy the way things were for another six months. After that, if Jeremy still was unsure about commitment, she said she would have to move on. Both wanted their lovemaking to resume as normal, and with the air cleared they were ready to try some sensual exercises. In the meantime Jeremy got a full medical that gave him the 'all clear', and spoke to his manager about how best to reach his targets at work. Jeremy reported feeling much better and more confident about life now that his real feelings were in the open.

Sensual Exercises

Anyone experiencing difficulty maintaining an erection should get a medical check first to rule out any physical problems. After that, it is important when there have been erection difficulties in a relationship that the couple takes a step back to remove the pressure from lovemaking. Try these sensual exercises in the following order.

Conjuring sensual memories

In order to shake off negative images that may now enter either the man's thoughts or both their thoughts, it is a good idea to relax and conjure up sensual memories from past lovemaking. The first step is to do this together, quietly cuddling, each with your private memories. Then once both of you feel confident of the memories you have recalled, each should describe some of their sensual memories. Lovemaking is not to follow this. Simple cuddles and sensual stroking will do at this stage.

Emphasizing the erotic

The next step to regaining 'erectile' confidence is to emphasize to each other all the positive erotic things you each do, which of course links with 'sensual memories'. Too many couples focus on what the other is doing wrong or not doing. Emphasizing the erotic is important to building sexual confidence. Too often we enjoy a sexual moment but let it pass without letting our lover know how good

they made us feel. Sometimes describing such moments verbally feels quite threatening for a couple trying to reclaim their sex life. If this is the case, you might start by agreeing to describe briefly just one thing your lover does that always feels good. For example, you may say you love the way they use their tongue in a French kiss. This may seem insignificant but to the person receiving the praise it is not – it reaffirms them as a lover.

Technique perfection

Select one sensual technique each. Selection should be on the basis that you love giving it and your partner enjoys receiving it. Then see how you can vary the technique to develop your sensuality and gain more sexual confidence. For example, you might tell your lover it feels fabulous the way he massages your inner thigh. He then experiments by varying his technique. Perhaps for a few minutes he gently nuzzles or kisses where he normally strokes. Perhaps he adds some sort of lubricant to slide up and down your inner thigh. The choices are endless and there is so much opportunity for pleasure in this non-threatening experimentation.

Sensual pathways dreamercise

Jeremy tried this dreamercise (*see page 34*) to develop dreams in which his erection would grow and grow to satisfying dimensions.

Having Sex to Gain Affection

"I was lying on a grassy mound, enjoying the warm feeling of the sun.
I wore an unusual dress that was wrapped around me like an Indian sari. A man
approached me and, without speaking, he reached out to me. I wanted to get up but
couldn't find my feet. It felt really odd that I couldn't stand up to meet him.
My hand could reach his and as our hands touched I pulled him to the ground.
The next thing I knew we were kissing passionately and he was slowly
unwrapping my strange dress. The sky was getting darker, like nightfall
approaching. I was getting aroused and couldn't wait for him to get through the
layers. He stroked between my legs, through the material, as the wrappings of the
dress simply didn't seem to end. Suddenly his erection poked through his trousers.
It seemed really out of place and I started to cry. Through my weeping
I was saying, 'I didn't want that!'"

Background and Interpretation

Linda's present relationship was very physical. Linda had been seeing Sam for four weeks. She had slept with him on the first night and the whole affair seemed to revolve around landing in bed. They never went out. Linda felt Sam was a good lover but the affair seemed to have a life of its own. It was based on sex and she could already guess that it would fizzle out soon. This had happened to Linda all too often during recent years.

What Linda actually wanted was to share her life with someone, not just her bed.

She had always been very independent – maybe too independent, she now feared. Why else did her relationships never extend beyond between the sheets? When she was younger, just sex seemed fine. Now she wanted love, warmth and stability. However, because of her independence, she had never been good at communicating her needs appropriately. Secretly she hoped that diving into bed would somehow lead to a more rounded relationship. The dream sent alarm bells ringing in her head.

ANALYSING LINDA'S DREAM

Linda's overtly sexual dream contains many symbols. The grassy mound and pleasant sunny dreamscape when she is on her own indicate contentment within herself. Her natural sensuality is apparent in her enjoyment of the sun on her body. Noticing her unusual dress is the first indication of her deeper feelings. The dress seems alien to Linda and yet it 'protects' her from having a full sexual encounter with the stranger. Her subconscious uses this image to say, 'Ensure he unwraps every bit of you and gets to know you slowly before you become physically acquainted with him.'

The arrival of the stranger to whom she immediately reaches out is symbolic of her habit of allowing men to get physically intimate too quickly. The fact that he does not speak reflects how Linda does not allow the men she meets to open up to her – another important message from her subconscious. Not being able to 'find her feet' symbolizes how she has been unable to take one step at a time in her relationships. In fact, she has generally allowed herself to be swept away by a new lover rather than deliberately pacing the relationship.

As darkness falls, the man attempts to unwrap her. The sunny aspect is being replaced by a darker emotion. The unwrapping represents reaching for her inner self, except that he never manages it. He does not discover the real her, just as men do not in her waking life. All she gives of herself is her sexual arousal. She has a feeling of enjoyment as he strokes her but this changes abruptly when his erection 'pokes out' from his trousers. Poking out from nowhere reveals how dissatisfied she is with simply having men's penises on offer. Finally, the crying, and saying aloud, 'I didn't want that!' reveals the deep disappointment she feels at the lack of emotional depth in her relationships.

RESOLVING THE ISSUES

In talking about the dream, Linda accepts that all the signals she gives out to the men she meets are sexual when what she really craves is affection and love. Sex has become her bartering chip for warmth. Now she must learn to make an emotional connection as well as a sexual one. Linda thinks Sam has many good qualities and hopes that acting on her dream's message will enable her to develop a meaningful relationship with him rather than it being yet another unsatisfying, short-lived fling.

Overleaf the exercises that Linda tried are described in full.

Sensual Exercises

Learning to reach out for emotional connection in a sexual relationship is an important step to take. By attaining emotional depth you will also develop your sensuality. Try these exercises:

Checking signals

If you give sex when you want affection you are probably talking too frequently about sexual topics to lovers, telling too many sexual jokes, making innuendos and doing too much sexual touching.

Run your most recent date like a film in your mind. Be honest with yourself. Did you exhibit any or some of the behaviours listed? Learn to use these sorts of behaviours more sparingly.

Developing foreplay

Sometimes emotional connection is achieved during foreplay. As foreplay develops so too does the opportunity for an emotional bond. As well as touching, kissing and other sensual techniques, some conversation may develop. This can be playful conversation about each other's bodies or it may contain some emotional content. For example, you may flirtatiously tell your partner that they are the only one you have allowed to touch you in a certain place or in a certain way. Or you may pay them intimate compliments, telling them how they make you feel extremely comfortable in a way that no one else ever has. Such affectionate foreplay can increase your confidence in opening up to a lover with whom, until now, you have been purely physical.

Identifying a need for affection

Learning to read your own moods will help you develop more depth to your sexual relationships. If you are upset or stressed and fall into bed, you are likely to be having sex simply to gain affection. You need to be absolutely confident, particularly early in a relationship, that it is sex you want and not just a hug. Ask yourself the following three questions. If you answer 'Yes' to all of them, then draw the line at jumping into bed: sex will not satisfy you.

1 Do you feel you want comfort from your partner?
2 Do you feel unable to tell them about what has happened in your day and want them to guess?
3 Would you actually be just as happy to be with a close friend/relative instead of your new lover?

Emotional disclosure

Disclosing personal information about yourself should take place one step at a time if you have a tendency to use sex for affection. Allowing gradual disclosure will feel less threatening. Disclosure can be about sexual or emotional topics. Take a piece of paper and draw a pyramid. Starting from the bottom of the pyramid write down the most basic piece of personal information or topic you would feel comfortable sharing with a new lover. This might be your feelings about your best friend's boyfriend (he's a pain). Above this enter the next topic that would take slightly more trust to talk about perhaps your dislike of your next-door neighbour who is always dropping in unannounced. Work up to the top of the pyramid with topics that gradually get more personal. The next topic, for example, might be how in your last job you experienced unwanted advances from your boss. At the top of the pyramid may be something you have never shared with a lover.

By drawing a 'disclosure pyramid' you clarify the issues that are important to you and prioritize them. Use this as a guide to the kinds of feelings and thoughts you gradually introduce to your lover. It will help map the way for you. With each topic ask whether they have had similar experiences.

Deeper emotional connection

Now you may be ready to talk about your emotional needs to your lover. Choose a moment when you are both relaxed; do not choose a time when one of you has rushed in stressed! Start with an 'I' statement to personalize what you are saying. Many people who have trouble with emotional connection talk as though they are describing someone else. They may say, 'You know how some people feel that they may never find the right person ...' rather than, 'I've felt at times that I may never find the right person to settle down with...' Being clear in a calm moment is the most positive way to expressing what you have been feeling.

Losing Desire for Sex

"I was walking down a corridor that didn't have any windows – it was a bit suffocating. I heard voices in the distance and found my way to them. I eventually came across what seemed to be an orgy. Men and women were writhing together on the floor. There seemed to be breasts, bottoms and genitalia everywhere. It was hot and stuffy and I felt 'different' because I was the only one with clothes on. People looked up at me as I passed through and I tried to ignore them. Suddenly my wife appeared, naked, with a man on her arm. She acted like this was perfectly normal. They started caressing each other. I shouted at her, 'What on earth are you doing?' She replied, 'I'm just going about my business.' I felt very angry. Everything faded into the distance and then I woke up feeling unhappy and angry."

Background and Interpretation

Tony was disturbed by this sexual dream. He had been married to Sarah for five years. When they first dated, Sarah took the sexual lead as she was far more experienced than he was. Tony had lost his virginity in a furtive one-night stand only a year before they met, and had gained little sexual knowledge since then.

He was consequently eager but inexperienced. They enjoyed tremendous lovemaking, Sarah skilfully showing him some of the many sophisticated sexual practices she loved. After they married they maintained a fairly active sex life. Tony particularly enjoyed the gentle bondage Sarah had introduced him to. And Sarah loved his 'oral eagerness' as she called it laughingly – he was always ready to satisfy her in this way.

Over the years they had slipped into a routine in which Sarah initiated sex. Her sex drive remained fairly constant but both of them started to suspect that Tony was losing interest. It was a subject neither found easy to discuss. Sex had been so easy from the start, why make a problem of a little lack of interest now? they both privately reasoned. Increasingly Tony felt worse. Sometimes he was angry with himself for losing interest. At other times he was angry with Sarah, whom he deemed 'insatiable'. At these moments he was prone to lash out at her.

ANALYSING TONY'S DREAM

The symbolism in Tony's dream is very clear. Walking down the suffocating corridor represents his feelings towards Sarah. The corridor itself symbolizes her sexuality generally, and her vagina more specifically, and her 'insatiable' appetite. The length of it symbolizes his sense of their 'endless' problem: they have been avoiding discussing his lack of sexual interest for some months now. He feels suffocated as he does in real life by his feeling of not living up to the sexual expectations raised early in their relationship. Making his way towards the 'voices' is Tony's subconscious pushing him to explore beyond the corridor. When he encounters the orgy he feels 'different'. He is quite removed from the activities as he is above the participants, who are looking up at him. This indicates how judged he feels about his loss of desire he is not one of them, someone who enjoys sex.

Tony tries to ignore the people having sex despite being acutely aware of what they are doing. This mirrors his attitude in waking life: not openly acknowledging that he has a problem while knowing that he has. Seeing Sarah naked with another man represents his subconscious fear that she will go elsewhere for sex because he is not satisfying her. Sarah's reply that she is 'going about her business' evokes anger in him because it stresses her view of sex as 'normal'. This again confirms his lack of desire, making him feel inadequate. Everything 'fading into the distance' is Tony's subconscious reminding him that the whole situation has gone beyond his control. His anger on waking simply reflects the inner anger he has about this problem, which has largely been ignored.

RESOLVING THE ISSUES

Loss of sexual desire can create many conflicting feelings. The person may feel insecure, angry at themselves and angry with their partner, all at the same time. These uncomfortable feelings are hard to face but if they are swept under the carpet they simply grow and fester. Tony and Sarah realized that they now had to face up to the changes in their sexual relationship. In many men, as with Tony, loss of desire may be completely unrelated to erection difficulties. Tony could get erect but the initial desire to make love was becoming increasingly rare. Very often whole lifestyle and/or relationship issues are involved in loss of desire. Awareness of these issues needs to be raised before looking at how to increase desire.

Sensual Exercises

Lifestyle exploration

Take the time to sit down together and look at your lifestyle. It may help to each draw two sets of 'lifestyle circles', one set representing how you actually spend your time and the other representing how you would ideally like to spend your time. For the first set draw several concentric circles. In the inner circle write down what you spend the most time doing; for example, work, study or childcare. In the next circle out write down what you spend your second largest amount of time on; then your third, and so on. Include work, leisure activities, childcare (if you have children), practical activities (chores, errands), 'intimate relationship' and

friends/family in your circles. In the second set of 'lifestyle circles' write down how you would like to divide your time. Then consider how the actual circles can become the desired set. Make long- and short-term goals to help you achieve your aims.

Often those who suffer from lessening sexual desire have a great deal of re-prioritizing to do in their lives in order to create the time and energy to feel sexually alive again. For example, you may decide that it would be beneficial to you as a couple to cut down on time spent doing overtime at work (and have less money to spend) and instead devote more time to being together enjoying each other and rekindling sexual feelings.

Related Themes

Secretly watching others making love

This dream imagery suggests that you are hiding from your true sexual desires. Think back over the scene you enjoyed watching in your dream – perhaps you can incorporate the sexual practices featured in it in your lovemaking.

Being watched while having sex

Such a dream reveals that you long to be less inhibited in your sexual relationship. It is time to break free of negative sexual 'habits', such as sexual inhibition, in front of your lover.

Participating in an orgy

Such a dream image may be standard wish fulfilment of a fantasy you have and realize you would be unlikely to act out. A word of warning to anyone considering dabbling in the 'swinging scene': be sure group sex is what you really want. Fantasy is usually far better than reality. Never be coerced by a partner into participating in group sex. If you are happy to try it, then insist on using condoms and agree some grounds rules about the sorts of sexual practices you will engage in before you start.

Recapture initial desires

During a quiet moment together (preferably over a candlelit dinner) take turns describing to your lover what initially excited you about the other. Be as graphic and detailed as you like. Remembering your initial sexual attraction to one another can help rekindle such feelings.

Recreate erotic success

Each select an erotic experience you had together and agree to recreate what happened. Perhaps you went for a picnic and ended up having al fresco sex under a clear blue sky. Take the time to retrace your steps. Enjoy the moment together, recapturing sexual 'successes' of the past.

Wish fulfilment

Agree to share one secret desire with each other. What have you privately wanted to try with your lover? Fulfilling each other's wishes will have a very positive affect on desire.

Sensual you dreamercise

Tony used this imaginative technique (*see page 32*) just before he fell asleep to shape dreams in which he enjoyed a lustful sexual appetite.

Exerting
Sexual Control

"I was lounging around in pyjamas (which really irritates my girlfriend) when Marina walked in, wearing a coat. I beckoned her to sit by me and started kissing her passionately. She was chattering away, which annoyed me. Marina carried on and I started kissing down her coat. I could feel the woolly texture on my lips, which I quite enjoyed. I got to the coat belt and pulled it. It grew longer and I wrapped it around and around her body. Between the belt I could see her breasts and labia poking through. I was very aroused by this and was trying to stroke them. Marina suddenly said: 'You never pay attention to my coat!' The dream ended without sexual fulfilment."

Background and Interpretation

S erge and Marina had been together for six tumultuous months. The difficulties in the relationship were mainly due to his sexual attitudes. Serge had experienced difficulties in the sexual side of his relationships in the past and now it was happening again. He could not stop linking his own sexual gratification to the rest of the relationship. Serge also tended to use sex as an emotional weapon – if he could get his way in the bedroom then he usually managed to get his way out of it, too. Marina felt that he was trying to control her in the relationship. By pressurizing her to match both his sexual appetite and his need for sexual experimentation, he seemed to be exerting control over the rest of the relationship. She was trying to stand up to this pressure and maintain the rela-

tionship because Serge had his good points, too. For one thing, he was extremely intelligent, and she felt he stimulated her intellectually. But both intellects could not seem to work out how to handle the raw emotion of the bedroom.

ANALYSING SERGE'S DREAM

Serge's dream begins with him lounging in his pyjamas, something he knows irritates Marina because he often asks for caresses through the pyjama opening and she always says he wants

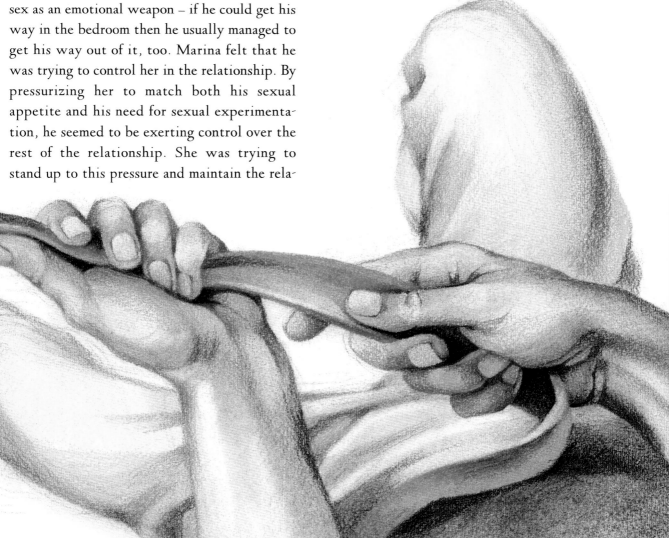

sex on demand. This establishes his sense of being 'right' in his ways. Marina enters wearing a coat, representing his belief that she always plays hard to get. The annoyance he feels as he tries to kiss Marina, and she simply chatters, reflects the irritation he often feels in waking life that she is not focusing enough on his needs. Serge ignores Marina's chattiness and kisses her coat instead. Enjoyment of the woolly texture symbolizes his enjoyment of giving her oral sex regardless of her enjoyment or even awareness.

Pulling Marina's coat belt is a clear symbol of how he tries to pull her into his way of doing things in waking life. By wrapping it around her, his subconscious is demonstrating how he would like to have her all wrapped up within his grasp. It is a symbol of his wish to control her so that quite literally she cannot move. The exposure of her most private parts – and Serge's arousal at this – symbolizes how he distances himself from her as a person. His subconscious shows how he is quite happy enjoying her breasts and labia without thought of her as a

whole. But Marina proves elusive in the dream: in waking life she is not going to simply roll over and let him do what he wants. Her saying, 'you never pay attention to my coat' is his subconscious protecting him from the harsh fact that she feels he never pays attention to her real feelings. The coat is an unusual symbol for these feelings and the gulf they cause between them.

RESOLVING THE ISSUES

Serge feels that Marina does not do enough to meet his needs and Marina believes he is far too controlling in their sexual relationship. Accusations fly easily between them, making it hard for them to move beyond this. Both need to find ways of handling their sexual and emotional conflicts more healthily. Anyone who tries to use sex as a means of control in a relationship needs to relearn how to relate to the other person. They need to realize that their sexual relationship is not a series of rewards for good behaviour and that it should not be used to control the other.

Sensual Exercises

Learning to express emotions

Serge needed to be able to tell Marina how he felt about different issues rather than take it out on her in the bedroom with sexual demands. He started by writing down feelings about her and their relationship in a small diary as they occurred. The two of them then took time to look at these together. Having his feelings in writing in a private

diary helped Serge to go on to discuss them. Marina was then able to describe how the diary entries made her feel and to discuss their subject matter.

Learning to negotiate

Marina wanted to feel that her sexual moods and needs counted in the relationship. She wanted Serge to accept her at her word if she was not in the mood or did not like his suggestions about trying something new. She did not want to have to justify her feelings. She also wanted Serge to stop sneering at her suggestions, as he had in the past, calling them too romantic or silly. If she wanted him to give her a sensual massage, then he was to try it.

Sensual healing

It is very healing to let go of a feeling that something must be proved in the bedroom, or that relationship power must be won there. Serge practised visualizations of himself relaxing in sensual surroundings, enjoying the moment rather than thinking ahead to how this would 'throw' or affect her. His aim was to enjoy the moment with no ulterior motives. Serge particularly enjoyed visualizing giving oral sex to Marina without thinking, 'Now she owes me.' He could see how positive it was to take this pressure off himself.

Sensual pathways dreamercise

Serge used this dreamercise (*see page 34*) to create a scene in which he strolled down a beautiful path with Marina, enjoying a free, affectionate bond. He imagined a dream ending with carefree lovemaking in which they were both equally involved.

Related Themes

Being 'wrapped up' by someone or something in a sexual dream

If the sensation accompanying this image is pleasurable, then you may like to take a more submissive role in lovemaking. If it evokes an uncomfortable feeling, then you may feel your lover is trying to control you – literally by wrapping you up and preventing movement during the sexual content of the dream.

Body parts being exposed in different ways

If it is your own body parts being exposed to another person (rather than looking at your lover's as in Serge's dream), and you experience pleasure in the dream, it suggests that you would like to expose more of your sensual self to them. If your body is being flaunted in front of others and you feel anxious, then you are under sexual pressure in your relationship.

Wearing attire that stands out from others in some way

If in your dream you are dressed and others are naked, you are feeling detached from your sexual relationship. You are the odd one out. If you experience a longing to strip off these clothes you are indicating your willingness to develop your sexual relationship at this time or alternatively that you are currently in a period of sexual development and acceptance.

Addicted to Sex

"I was in a restaurant with some girlfriends. One of the women, whom I didn't know, whispered to me about 'the party' going on in the back room. Suddenly I was following her into a private room where a cocktail party was in full throttle. No one looked up as we entered and I said to her, 'Will they know we're gatecrashers?' This was ignored and the next thing I knew a man had taken me by the waist and had started fondling me. I accepted his caresses without question. He backed me on to a table and slipped inside me. He was thrusting like a stallion and it was over within seconds. I wandered over to another man who looked at me lustfully. Again I succumbed to his caresses — it was as if I was on heat. I felt insatiable. He pulled me to the floor and we rolled over and over in a heated sexual embrace. I looked up and grinned at another man who was watching. Then the woman who'd led me in said to me, 'Don't you have any taste?' I felt so offended and cut to my very core."

Background and Interpretation

Alexis has rarely managed to maintain a relationship past the 'fling' stage. She has recently had a string of one-night stands that have left her feeling emotionally drained. In fact, she feels worthless and disconnected. And yet she keeps going back to the nightclub scene for more. Alexis has complained to her closest friend that she should not feel drained when it has 'only been sex, after all'. She has failed to link her sexual behaviour to her emotional needs. Now she feels it is time to think before she jumps into bed again. She knows this is going to be difficult as when she is out with friends, even when they try to discourage her, she finds it extremely hard to stop herself from looking around for a little 'man-action', as she jokes. She can see that the message of her dream is linked to the feelings she has after the flings.

ANALYSING ALEXIS'S DREAM

The restaurant setting represents the social side of Alexis's nature. Restaurant themes are common in the dreams of sociable people. This side of her nature has led her to look for the attention and excitement she craves in inappropriate ways. The strange woman who whispers to her symbolizes the part of her emotional self that has abandoned any normal constraints. This risk-taking aspect of herself is expressed sexually. Alexis happily follows the woman into the party, but the more sensitive side of Alexis's nature tries to make itself felt when she asks about being spotted as 'gatecrashers'. She does have a conscience and she does not want to be seen as a gatecrasher or, more specifically, she does not want to be perceived as an 'easy lay'.

Allowing the first man to take her by the waist and take over sexually indicates her loss of control in sexual encounters – Alexis is allowing men to do things to her rather than with her. The powerful image of 'thrusting like a stallion' reveals how animal and basic her flings have become. It is over in seconds, reflecting the short-lived nature of them. Next Alexis succumbs to another man – just as she does in waking life – symbolizing her lack of control. Feeling 'insatiable' symbolizes how deep her sexuality runs. However, it has not been tempered with caution for her emotional well-being. The overall symbolism of the sexual imagery taking place at the party reveals a deeper sense that what she is doing will be judged in some way by others. And the final question about having 'any taste' is a padded blow from her subconscious. She avoids saying to herself 'aren't you acting like a slut?' but Alexis is in no doubt when she wakes up as to the deeply symbolic nature of the remark.

RESOLVING THE ISSUES

Alexis has been coasting through her one-night stands with little thought for her well-being. Although she complains they leave her with negative feelings, she has failed to understand why – that this cycle of empty sexual encounters has a cumulative effect on her self-esteem. Understanding why she craves attention and/or risk, and seeks it through unhealthy sexual behaviour, is the first step she needs to take.

With careful analysis Alexis came to understand some of the emotional demons driving her sexually addictive behaviour. She understood that the risk-taking behaviour helped guard against facing up to the realities of her life. Also that the intense attention she received during the sexual act was pleasurable, but that it left an immense void. She then sought even more intense sexual activity to fill this void, which left her with even more negative feelings. She realized that she needed to break this cycle.

Sensual Exercises

Someone who has struggled with sex addiction or addictive-type behaviours needs to learn to understand that emotional connection for them needs to come first. That emotional connection may lead to more sensually satisfying relationships.

Taking time

Allowing time to get to know yourself at a sensual level, and another person, actually enhances sensuality rather than detracting from it. Rushed, 'animal' sex may have its place in lovemaking but not until the sex addict has gained control over their compulsive behaviour. You need to accept that you have time to explore your own sexual responses, having identified any negative sexual behaviours that impact on your emotional well-being.

Self-knowledge may be gained through sensual masturbation in a relaxed moment. Explore your body carefully to find out what arouses you. With your next lover take the time with sensual massage and foreplay to gain a real knowledge of their body, not a rushed glimpse.

Learning to take control

Being guided by sexual impulses rather than controlling them may lead to unfulfilling encounters. You need to take control of sexual encounters so that they occur with someone you want to have sex with, at a time you want to have sex, and not simply to gain affection or attention. People who have addictive tendencies find it hard to put the brakes on the development of sexual relationships so that they occur at a pace they are truly happy with.

If this sounds like you, take one day at a time and set a goal for your next encounter; for example, decide that you will not engage in sexual activity until you are sure you actually care for the person and they for you. Always listen to your instincts. If they tell you that a person is 'in it for the sex', believe that message. Ignore the impulses you may feel to prove yourself wrong or to try to 'capture' this elusive person. Think about where you have met previous sexual partners – in nightclubs and bars? Plan to meet people socially in environments not geared to 'pick ups' and fuelled by alcohol – sports, leisure activities and further education classes are far preferable. Do not get into situations where you will be under pressure to have sex that you are not ready for; for example, avoid going to a new partner's house or your own with them, if no one else will be around. A smooch on the sofa can so easily lead to full sex.

Seeking risk elsewhere

To help temper a need for taking sexual risks, identify other, non-destructive ways of finding excitement in your life. These may include action sports, or taking part in amateur performing arts. Once you have established a full relationship with a lover you may then wish to introduce some exciting sexual activities to spice up your sex life if you both desire it *(see the sensual exercises on pages 74–5)*.

Sensual beginnings dreamercise

Alexis used this dreamercise *(see page 33)* to promote dreams in which she laughed and talked with others, enjoying herself in social situations without plunging into sexual activity.

Handling Frustrated Desire

"I found myself in the midst of a thundering herd of horses. Their hooves were pounding the earth so hard that my entire body was quivering. I could not count the number of horses but I had a sense that I was surrounded. My heart was beating quickly and I felt very excited. I tried to jump on to one but my grip loosened and I slipped off. I tried to grab another by its mane and once again I slipped. At this point there was no fear, I just longed to 'be' with one of them. Then I realized they were heading for a cliff. With mounting anxiety I watched as they tumbled off one by one. I could not see the ground at the bottom of the cliff but I knew they must be hitting it. They appeared to go over in slow motion and my anxiety rose as I called to those remaining to prevent them from taking the fatal plunge."

Background and Interpretation

This dream was described by Fiona, who has been with her lover for five years. In the last year their sexual relationship has deteriorated. She is still attracted to her lover but he seems uninterested. Their style of lovemaking is in a rut, which Fiona finds frustrating. Although she describes the rest of their relationship as 'good' she is worried that he is bored, as she is, and might stray. She has tried experimenting in their lovemaking, hoping to hit upon the role that appeals to her lover: she has played the 'vamp', the sexual aggressor and the 'ice maiden'. Fiona is unhappy that all efforts to improve their sex life stem from her energies.

ANALYSING FIONA'S DREAM
Horses are classic symbols in sexually charged dreams, with many veiled meanings. Fiona's

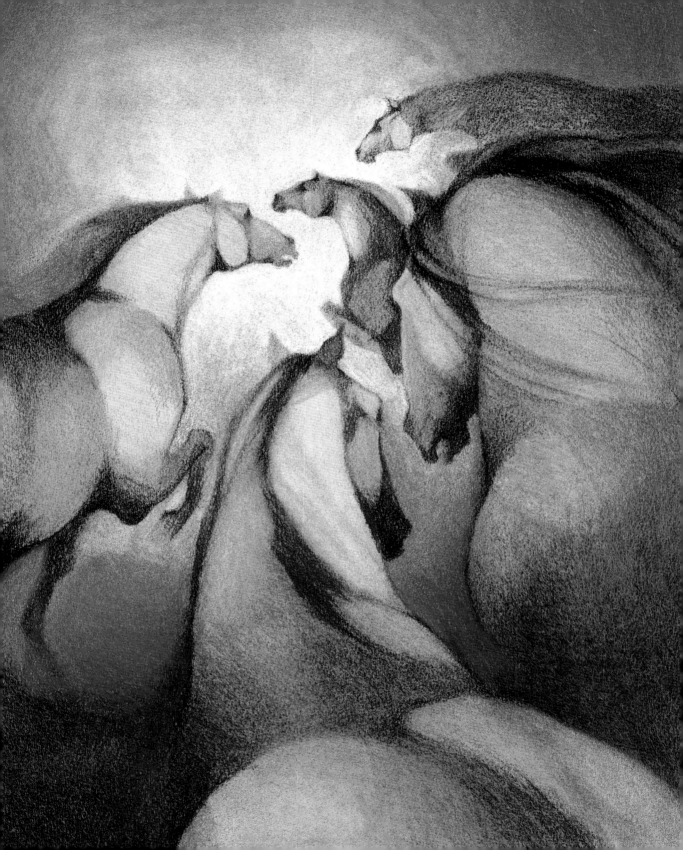

dream contains contrasting feelings and themes. It begins with the sense of being surrounded by strong sexuality, which represents her unbridled passion for her lover. The dream changes as she tries to climb on to a horse but fails. This symbolizes her sense of rejection by her partner, yet the failure raises her desire to try again. The number of horses signifies the many roles she has tried to improve their sex life. When Fiona's desire to ride quickly turns to fear, the tumbling horses represent the way she feels about her attempts to try to excite her partner. Her hopes tumble into oblivion. Calling out shows her desire to communicate – she will not give up. The cliff symbolizes the ultimate level of her anxiety: she does not allow herself to 'see' what happens to the horses. This is a protective mechanism. Subconsciously she knows that their sexual relationship is crumbling but she does not want to face this consciously. She contains her anxiety by making sure she does not know for certain what happens to the horses.

RESOLVING THE ISSUES

When your subconscious 'sees' that your sex life is heading for trouble you may consciously seek to avoid facing the problem by acting in unhelpful ways that either confuse the issue or worsen the situation. Casting herself in different sexual roles is clearly causing Fiona deep unhappiness and making the problem worse. Fiona is not naturally an 'actress'. By role playing during sex, without telling her lover what is going on, she is probably unnerving him. As he has a naturally reserved sexual style, such contrasting 'performances' are leading him to fall back on his tried and tested sexual routines, thus frustrating Fiona.

Fiona is now working on improving her communication skills to allow her to express her needs without threatening her rather reserved partner. Her confidence is developing and she understands that a disparity in sexual styles may yield pleasing results when tackled from a position of honesty and openness.

Sensual Exercises

Putting your lover centre stage

If you have a reserved lover, then building their confidence may help them to communicate more openly with you. Try describing to them a sexual fantasy in which they play the central character. This will make them feel valued and will also help them to see erotic potential initiated by you but involving them. You could try writing out your fantasy and leaving it as a 'love note'.

Flights of fantasy

The next step to increasing a sense of adventure between the two of you is to discuss fantasies that involve others. For example, you might like to include a famous person in a fantasy scenario (*see Eric's film star fantasy, page 116*), or a make-believe phantom lover. Be playful and take turns describing your fantasy. Reassure one another that fantasizing about others is only a part of your fantasy life.

Role playing

You can push back the boundaries further by acting out a fantasy scene. For example, you might play the role of the 'demanding' boss. Your lover has made a big mistake in his work and you take him to task, telling him the only way he can make it up to you is to become your sexual plaything. The possibilities are endless. Role play comes to life when you act out different personalities, taking different names and wearing different clothes for each part.

Related Themes

Riding a horse

Riding is often very rhythmic with the rider experiencing sexual arousal and feeling at one with a powerful horse. This signifies satisfaction with your present relationship. At a deeper level it represents sexual confidence: you are happy to accept pleasure when it comes your way.

Thrown by a horse

Being thrown by a horse in a dream can represent your subconscious feelings for your lover. At a conscious level, you may be aware that you do not quite trust your lover or their level of commitment. The act of being thrown from the horse is a subconscious message urging you to listen to your doubts.

A horse that bolts

This can signify subconscious fears that you either want to run away from your relationship or that you have grave worries that your lover is about to drop you. Such dreams are often accompanied by sexual tension. The subconscious can pick up and 'read' subtle clues given by a lover. It sees that the relationship is not working long before your conscious mind acknowledges this. The conscious mind clings to hope, suppressing fear.

Stroking a horse

This action in a dream is symbolic of the pleasure you derive from foreplay. Stroking the horse signifies your desire for tactile stimulation and affection. It may represent your need for more of this behaviour. If you are not presently involved with someone it may represent the void in your life. Stroking the horse is symbolic of stroking yourself – there should be no guilt in pleasuring yourself through masturbation.

Nuzzled by a horse

Deriving sexual pleasure in a dream from being nuzzled by a horse may indicate that you enjoy a passive role in lovemaking. This is fine as long as your lover enjoys taking the lead. Try to ensure that your lover does not tire of shouldering this responsibility for your pleasure.

Bored by Lover's Technique

"I was in the house I share with my partner, Gerry. Everything was
a dull grey – so unlike our real paintwork in our home, which is bright and lively.
As we were talking I started to heap some flour-like substance on him. He wanted
me to stop but I disregarded him completely and kept piling this stuff on. There
was so much it was cascading to the floor around his feet. I felt very frustrated,
turned and went to the back door. The garden was looking beautiful and I called
to Gerry to come and look with me. We walked out into the garden together and
again I started heaping some stuff on him. This time it was more like dirt than
flour. Then to my amazement Gerry started to sink down and disappear into the
garden. I was angry with him but he responded by saying, 'Well, you were trying to
bury me!' It was as if by sinking he was escaping from me."

Background and Interpretation

This dream was described by Francesca who had recently invested in a house with her partner, Gerry. After two years together they both thought of their relationship as long-term even though they had not really talked about marriage. Gerry sensed a resistance to marriage in Francesca, who was quite a free spirit, and he had never pushed for more commitment, although he would have liked their relationship to take a traditional path.

Gerry suspected that her reluctance to get married might be caused by the arguments they had periodically. These usually occurred after making love. He could not figure it out as he thought she enjoyed their sex life. In fact, Francesca was deeply bored with Gerry's skills as a lover. She loved his many other qualities and hoped he would become more inventive with time. Recently Francesca had taken to faking orgasm simply to get sex over with, which was something she had never done in the past. Somehow she felt Gerry would be deeply hurt if he knew the truth and she did not want to face that. She sometimes invoked her 'free spirit' attitude to avoid conflict.

ANALYSING FRANCESCA'S DREAM

The dull grey colouring of their home, so unlike their real home, is a clear symbol of Francesca's feelings about their sex life, which is overshadowed by a sense of dreariness. The greyness is further emphasized by the 'flour-like' substance she heaps over Gerry: flour is plain and lacklustre. Francesca is literally burying the displeasure she feels but cannot actually face in real life. The image of the flour cascading around his feet is suggestive of her view of his source of sexuality: at his feet and not in use. Suddenly turning and going to the back door symbolizes the way Francesca is turning her back on her frustration with her dull sex life.

Francesca's subconscious is trying to establish an invigorating source of pleasure by making the garden look so inviting. The fertile garden is a strong symbol of her desire to have her needs satisfied by a virile, or responsive, man. Her strongest subconscious emotion breaks through when Gerry sinks into the ground. Francesca sees him as hiding, or avoiding, such earthy, fertile possibilities. This image may also symbolize his lovemaking – he simply sinks into her in a very unsatisfactory way, making her angry. When Gerry says, 'you were trying to bury me', it is her subconscious recognizing that Gerry might also have feelings about their sexual relationship. So there is some guilt represented in her dream: she recognizes that if she is not honest with Gerry then she is 'burying' his chances to improve things.

RESOLVING THE ISSUES

Francesca must introduce more honesty into the sexual side of their relationship if the partnership is to survive in the long term. They are living together in a home they jointly own and openly acknowledge that this is a committed relationship for them both. Francesca realizes that something has to change and she accepts that her dream symbolizes, on one level, their loss of possibility – the possibility to make an improvement in their sex life.

Sensual Exercises

Sexual honesty

When people care deeply for their lover they often assume that honesty will hurt their partner more than 'faking it', and convince themselves that eventually, by some miracle, their sex life will improve as if by magic. With time, they may accept that this approach is not working and want to do something about it, but they cannot face going over old ground and owning up to the lying or half-truths they have already told about their sexual satisfaction. What they can do is choose a starting point for their new honesty. They can introduce the notion to their lover that they are *now* experiencing difficulty with desire, or arousal, or orgasm, and this is a new problem for them. This avoids their having to face the ramifications of previously having faked orgasm, or satisfaction in other ways. It is fine to say that things 'aren't quite working', or that you are 'feeling less relaxed' or simply that you would 'like to try some new techniques'.

Sexual bridging

There is always the possibility during an ongoing relationship that people's desires and/or needs change and differ. What may turn you on during one period of your relationship may not at another time. Our sexuality is fluid, not static. Every aspect of life affects your feelings, energy, desires and needs, and gaps may form between two previously close lovers. Such gaps can and should be bridged. The most positive way of handling any changes you experience is to reach out *as* and *when* they happen.

Letting your lover in on your changing needs reflects the depth of your relationship. As long as the bridging communication is done in a positive and caring spirit, it can only improve the quality of the relationship with your lover.

One of the easiest bridging methods is to use sensuality in the description of your needs or desires. For example, you may find that a comfortable position you have both loved in the past has lost its allure. As you and your lover caress each other in foreplay describe to them a new position or sexual practice you long to try. Let them know you have loved the 'old favourites' but that the new position will perhaps stimulate your clitoris, for example, in an optimal way. Or 'let your fingers do the talking' and lead your lover into a new position, or new speed of fingering, or secret place that you wish them to caress.

Sensual tutoring

Sometimes one of you is a more skilled lover than the other. This may be because one of you has had more experience because there is an age difference or because one has had a greater variety of partners than the other, or it may simply be because one of you has more sexual confidence than the other. If you feel that you are confident enough to lead the way in experimentation, then it is important to take an active role in developing your sex life, without ignoring the needs of your less experienced partner or treating them in a condescending manner. Sensual tutoring should be fun and not deadly serious! It should bring out the best in both of you.

As a sensual tutor you should always be willing to take sexual practices one step further. You might like to start with basic massage techniques. Perhaps you both love sensual massage in a warm, quiet room, and you are already practised at building up the swirling and stroking of your massage into actual foreplay. You could develop this further by introducing a sensual technique such as 'feathering'. Take a delicate feather, drizzle massage oil on to your partner and use the feather to swirl it down and around their erogenous zones.

Related Themes

Being buried as a pleasurable sensation

If you experience this sort of dream imagery it suggests that you would enjoy sex more if your lover took the sexual lead. Such imagery also suggests an earthiness in your sexual desires that would be fulfilled by some truly passionate lovemaking techniques.

Being buried accompanied by anxiety

This dream image suggests that you feel overwhelmed by either your lover's sexual demands or your own desires, which you have neglected. You quite literally feel as though you cannot move and are suffocated by what is happening in your sexual relationship.

Joining Sex with Love

"I was sitting in my office at work going through a pile of papers.
Some of my colleagues came up and said it was time for lunch. I explained that I
had work to do. My secretary said, 'Oh Raj, you're all work and no play!' as she
pulled out some hot dogs, burgers and chips. I protested, asking, 'Can't you see how
much I've got to do?' I was practically crying, which is odd because I never get
personal with people at work. The next thing I had a hot dog thrust in my hand
and a colleague was squeezing some ketchup on it from one of those plastic bottles.
It was gushing out. I said, 'Hang on, let me do my own!' and took the bottle. I
squeezed and squeezed but none would come out. Again I felt like crying.
I dropped the hot dog and pleaded with them to let me get back to work."

Background and Interpretation

Raj and Ali had been married for eighteen months and were having real difficulties in their sexual relationship. Both were deeply committed to their marriage and very much in love. Before they met, Raj had visited massage parlours for 'relief' as he termed it. Otherwise, he had only ever had one lover and that relationship had not been very successful. Ali had had a few love affairs at university and she had enjoyed the lovemaking she had experienced there. Sex with Raj had been a big disappointment. The first few weeks of marriage he had experienced premature ejaculation and after that he had not been able to ejaculate at all. At first Ali had assumed it was due to his sense of guilt over the premature ejaculation. Now she was at a loss to understand the cause of the problem.

It was getting harder and harder for either of them to even broach the subject. Raj was loathe to go to bed at night for fear Ali would approach him. He knew he had a big emotional 'block'. He could not reconcile the high esteem in which he held his wife and the 'pure love' he felt for her with the furtive, 'tainted' sex he had enjoyed in massage parlours in his late teens to mid-twenties. Raj felt that his ejaculation would in some ways 'taint' Ali and their relationship. And after the initial excitement of being in bed together immediately after the wedding, he simply could not 'let go' of his ejaculate. Raj knew these rather old-fashioned notions would surprise many and he felt Ali would not understand the conflicting feelings he had about love and sex.

ANALYSING RAJ'S DREAM

Raj did not link his unusual dream to his sexual relationship for quite a while because the setting was his workplace. He normally feels very comfortable at work and his natural efficiency means that he never has 'piles of paper' to get through. His subconscious chose the workplace for two reasons. Firstly, it serves as a protective mechanism – if the

dream had been set in his bedroom, it may have been too nightmarish for Raj to face. Secondly, it serves as a mild warning that his difficulties at home may impact on other areas of his life.

When his colleagues arrive, suggesting having lunch, Raj responds immediately by talking about his workload: he is trying to make sense of his avoidance of sex with Ali at home. In the dream he avoids the pleasure of sharing lunch. His secretary's response that he is 'all work and no play' is symbolic of how Raj believes Ali probably feels – that he is no fun in bed. Again, the message has been put gently.

The lunch selection is laid out and Raj nearly cries about the 'work to be done'. This is a message telling him he must face the work to be done – but at home, with his wife, not at work with his colleagues. Raj is given a hot dog from the selection – a clear symbol of the male erection. When his colleague holds the ketchup, it gushes out on to the plate but when Raj takes it he cannot manage to force anything from the bottle. This symbolizes his inability to ejaculate, and is distressing for Raj. He pleads for his colleagues' understanding, reflecting his underlying desire to share his worries and feelings with Ali. The degree of Raj's unhappiness is clear from his desire to weep.

RESOLVING THE ISSUES

Raj realizes that he risks the failure of his entire marriage if he does not face Ali with his deepest feelings and attitudes about sex, which of course directly impact on her pleasure as well as his own. Thinking about the dream made Raj aware that his inner self was suffering because he was hiding from his wife his sense that ejaculation would somehow 'tarnish' and 'sully' his love for Ali. In fact, their love was being tarnished by his dishonesty. Your physical response in love-making is directly influenced by your emotions and attitudes. And hiding your feelings may lead to unhappy or negative sexual experiences.

Sensual Exercises

Making associations

Learning to associate love with sex may be an important step if your sexual attitudes infringe on your sexual pleasure. Sit down with your partner and together list all the positive elements in your overall relationship. Such a list might include trust, emotional intimacy, meeting each other's needs and sharing 'problems'. Now list all the negative aspects of your relationship, such as withholding affection or attention, keeping secrets and being critical. Next, together examine and discuss the entries on the positive list to see how they relate to your emotional AND sexual behaviour as a couple. When you do this exercise it will soon become apparent, at least in principle, that sharing intimacy and meeting each other's needs provides a positive link between the sexual and emotional aspects of your relationship.

Visualizing positive images of sexual intimacy

Visualize a non-threatening lovemaking image; for example, one in which the two of you are kissing innocently. Now describe it to your partner. Next visualize the two of you kissing passionately, and describe that to your lover. Continue visualizing and describing progressively more intimate scenes until you reach an image featuring full intercourse.

If, before that, you encounter an image that makes either or both of you feel uncomfortable, stop the exercise for the moment. This indicates that you have reached a critical point for further work. For example, if you feel uncomfortable when your partner describes an image of the two of you caressing each other intimately, do not go any further. Only resume the exercise when your anxiety over this point has diminished.

Exploring your feelings

Building trust is imperative to learning to explore your feelings together. Trying to find 'sensual empathy' is one way of starting this process. Ask your lover to describe one of his sexual feelings or attitudes. Now put yourself in your lover's shoes and describe what you think he or she means. Your lover should respond by telling you how accurate you were. For example, Ali might describe to Raj what she thought he meant about his attitudes to sex being different depending on his feelings towards his lover. Take plenty of time and listen carefully to each other.

Final climax dreamercise

Raj used some of the suggestions in this dreamercise (*see page 35*) to shape dreams in which his ejaculation was powerful and pleasurable.

Related Themes

Endless pouring or gushing from a bottle

An image of a gushing liquid in your dream symbolizes your freedom within a sexual relationship to express yourself.

Inability to open a container

Being unable to force open a container symbolizes sexual frustration. The more you struggle, the deeper the frustration, either with your lover or with your own sexual performance.

Being presented with a feast

Being able to choose from a 'delicious feast' laid out before you in a dream symbolizes your joy in your present sexual relationship and in sexual matters generally.

If you do not have a lover at the moment, such an image of sumptuous delight indicates wish fulfilment on your part: you fervently desire to sample from a delicious platter, or feast, of sexual delights.

Aroused by Domination

"I was in a pub, which was the one I used to go to as a teenager. It was very dark and there were only a few people there. The publican looked a bit sleazy and I wanted to get away from him. I said I'd 'see to the beer barrels'. They were in the cellar, which was completely deserted but warm and comfortable. I felt I had to shift the barrels around and started to roll them across the floor. They moved easily. Some of them started leaking and I had to tighten the bindings around them. I was straining with the bindings – pulling them tight – and at the same time I felt aroused. I started to masturbate, stroking myself and surveying the work I had done. It was really strange: I was perched on a barrel all alone in that quiet cellar, enjoying sexual pleasure."

Background and Interpretation

Carrie had been seeing Jason for a few months. She was not sure how long the relationship would last as they had a few difficulties. Among these was her appetite for bondage techniques and Jason's inexperience in this area. Carrie definitely took the lead in their lovemaking and sometimes he was happy to go along with her wishes, as he was eager to please her. At other times, though, Jason would get very annoyed about always playing the same submissive role and complained that he wanted to enjoy 'normal sex', as he called it.

Jason was very drawn to Carrie's creative nature and strong personality, so his emotions seesawed. Carrie found it very difficult to reach orgasm without bondage being involved, so finding a compromise was difficult. She had been introduced to bondage in her first sexual

relationship with a slightly older man. It was an intense relationship and it had left her forever marked with the sense that sex was inextricably linked with domination and submission.

ANALYSING CARRIE'S DREAM
Carrie was surprised by her dream. Set in the pub of her teens, the dream reveals how deeply rooted Carrie's feelings are about her sexual needs and suggests that the way her sexual preferences developed is key. The pub is dark and quiet, symbolizing the sense of isolation Carrie feels with her sexual desires. She knows Jason does not really share her preferences.

The sleazy publican, who makes her feel uncomfortable, represents the man who introduced her to sex. Carrie has many unhappy memories of her relationship with this man, who she feels took advantage of her. Going to the cellar to 'see to the beer barrels' indicates her need to break away from the power of the publican to make her feel uncomfortable. Carrie finds comfort and warmth in the cellar and goes on to take control of the barrels by moving them around. This action fulfils her need to stay in control, or dominate, her surroundings. The barrels move easily, symbolizing how malleable Jason is. Next, she feels compelled to take charge of the leaks in the barrels. Straining with the bindings, she experiences pleasure and masturbates. This reveals her need for control and domination to gain sexual pleasure. The final dream image of being alone in the cellar surveying her work signifies her sense of being alone with her way of finding sexual release.

Resolving the issues

Carrie needed to take stock of the way her sexual preferences were dominating her relationship with Jason. Her dream clearly indicated that she needed to reconcile feelings from the past with the way she felt now. Carrie needed to gain control of her impulses to dominate if her relationship with Jason was going to become more pleasurable and less fraught.

How Sexually Dominant are You?

If you have wondered whether a need to be sexually dominant may be driving your sexual behaviour consider the following five questions. Each question has three optional answers. Score three points for each answer a); score two points for each answer b); score one point for each answer c).

1 *Do you feel compelled for any reason (for example, a sense of anxiety, or enthusiasm) to make the sexual advances early in a relationship?*
   a) Yes, I am almost always the first one to make sexual advances.
   b) I play my part in initiating a sexual relationship.
   c) No, I am unlikely to make sexual advances.

2 *Have you experienced relationship discord because a lover found you too controlling or dominant during sex?*
   a) Yes, I have had problems because of my sexual demands/expectations/practices.
   b) I have experienced some conflict/disagreement over what I would like my lover to do.
   c) No, I have not experienced this sort of problem.

3 *Are you sexually aroused by arguments or difficult emotions?*
   a) Yes, I am definitely aroused by passion within a relationship generally.
   b) Sometimes I get aroused after disagreements or difficult moments.
   c) No, I am not aroused by negative emotions.

4 *Do you only experience sexual fulfilment when engaged in submissive-dominant sexual practices or when 'in charge' sexually?*
   a) Yes, I enjoy being in charge.
   b) Sometimes that would be exciting.
   c) No, my sexual enjoyment is not dependent on such practices.

Sensual Exercises

Role reversal

If sexual pleasure is contingent upon always playing the same role, experiment with others. If you or your lover are aroused by dominance or submission, try reversing the roles to develop your sexual repertoire. Even if this simply becomes an exercise in sensual empathy it is good to try. It is particularly helpful if one of you objects to being pressurized into engaging in a particular sexual activity.

Compromise in sex play

If you or your lover objects absolutely to a particular sexual practice, then encourage sensual compromise. Consider the pleasures you could try that would be non-threatening to the objecting partner and satisfying to the other. For example, Carrie and Jason might reach compromise by agreeing not to use 'sub-dom' apparatus but to simply talk through a fantasy about submission and domination.

5 *Are you preoccupied with your own feelings during sex?*
  a) Yes, I am very aware of my own feelings and could not guess what my lover is feeling.
  b) I am more aware of my own feelings than my lover's during sex.
  c) No, I really want to be in touch with my lover's feelings.

It is important to understand that sexual dominance is not only about bondage and 'sub-dom' practices. You can be sexually dominant simply through the frequency with which you demand sex, your behaviour during sex, and the manner in which you approach your lover.

Score 11 to 15 points:
High Level of Sexual Dominance
You are likely at some point to run into opposition to, or unhappiness with, your dominant sexual attitudes. Such an attitude is fine if your lover enjoys your dominance, but perhaps they do not. Perhaps they simply go along with what you want, unable to express their true feelings to you. Ask your lover about your sex life. Reassure them you want them to be honest. Try the sensual exercises described above to enhance your sexual relationship.

Score 6 to 10 points:
Moderate Level of Sexual Dominance
You have a balanced approach to initiating or leading in your sexual relationships. You may wish to experiment with dominant and submissive role play or fantasy to enhance your sexual pleasure. However, you are not controlled by such a desire, simply open to the idea of experimentation.

Score 1 to 5:
No Sexual Dominance
You are not sexually dominant. In fact, you are likely to be sexually submissive. Do not allow your lover to dominate you sexually if that is not what you want. It is easy to go with the flow to please a lover but you must make sure you are also having your sexual needs met. Talk to your partner about your desires.

Withholding Sex as Punishment

"I was in our kitchen and everything was out of place.
I started to put things away. It seemed like an endless task and I was getting angry.
Then Elaine walked in and dropped her clothes in a pile on the floor. I asked her
why she was making a mess of everything. Elaine simply laughed and walked
around with no clothes on. The next thing I knew she bent over and I was looking
at her bottom. I didn't want her to know I was looking. I found some little cakes —
delicate things like you find in a real French patisserie. They had little swirls of
icing, flowers and tiny sugar shapes. I was determined to put them somewhere safe
from everyone, including Elaine; it went through my head that she might devour
them. I packed them away in airtight storage containers but did not really feel
happy with the job I had done. I awoke worrying about the little cakes."

Background and Interpretation

Alan and Elaine have been married for eight years. Alan has always used sex as an emotional 'tool' for punishing Elaine when he is angry or hurt. He achieves this by withholding sex from her. This used to lead to prolonged arguments between them, and many women would have left him or been 'beaten down' by his negative approach some time ago. However, Elaine has now found a way of dealing with his behaviour so that she is not hurt by it: she simply ignores it. If he chooses to fall into a bad mood and turn his back on her when she is in the mood for lovemaking, then she decides to read or watch television instead.

It is an unhappy arrangement but some would say that at least they have stopped arguing as a result. Unfortunately, when the arguing stops and an uneasy truce takes over, all communication between a couple may cease. Also, if you go to bed in a negative mood then you may well find it difficult to get to sleep or, if you do manage it, go on to suffer nightmares and a disturbed night's sleep.

ANALYSING ALAN'S DREAM

Alan felt uncomfortable when he awoke from his dream. It was located in the kitchen – the heart of their home – revealing how central the dream is to his feelings in general. Finding 'everything out of place' symbolizes anxiety, which is often at the root of veiled sexual dreams. Alan desperately wants the items in the kitchen to be ordered. When Elaine walks in and promptly drops her clothes on the floor she subverts this keenly felt desire.

Her action angers him for two reasons. Firstly, it seems almost as though she is trying to annoy him on purpose, which suggests that Alan thinks at some subconscious level that Elaine tries to get back at him, possibly for the way he withholds sex. Secondly, it symbolizes her natural approach to sex. She is open and fair-minded and does not withhold sex when she is angry or unhappy. Sex for her is quite simply sex, as straightforward as the dream image of her dropping her clothes.

Alan tries to peek at her exposed bottom, symbolizing the sneaky side of his nature that withholds sex when he is unhappy. Also, by trying to hide the fact that he is looking at her, he reveals some feelings of envy towards Elaine – possibly of the open way she handles relationship issues.

Coming across the tiny pastries reveals Alan's concern with detail and with 'feminine' things. He wants to lock them away. He does not want to enjoy the pastries or to let Elaine see them. Instead he forces them into airtight containers, indicating how deeply concerned he is with keeping things under control: sensual delights are there to be withheld from enjoyment. The final message from his subconscious – worrying about the cakes – is that he should be concerned about the way he treats Elaine. It is a veiled warning, as so often subconscious messages are.

RESOLVING THE ISSUES

Alan's dream is a 'wake-up call', drawing his attention to the negative emotions he experiences that lead him to withhold sex from Elaine, and to the impact of his actions on the relationship. Alan is putting his relationship with Elaine at serious risk by continuing to withhold sex as punishment. For, once one area of a relationship becomes off limits as far as real communication is concerned (in the case of Alan and Elaine, their sex life), then another area soon follows, and then another, until before you know where you are there is nothing of any personal importance that you can talk about. In addition, with her positive nature, Elaine may find that the attention of other men becomes tempting if her sexual frustration mounts.

Sensual Exercises

If you recognize that you withhold sex from your lover because of other negative feelings you have about them, try some or all of the exercises described below.

Sensual focus

If you tend to use sex as a punishment (which is what withholding is) you need to learn to focus on sex for its sensual pleasures. You must learn to distance other feelings, unrelated to lovemaking, from intimate behaviour with your lover.

Firstly, after lovemaking, cherish the moment, and do not allow any thoughts of other issues, problems or annoyances to slip into your mind. If they do so, stop them straight away by re-imaging the sexual sensations you have just experienced. Secondly, when annoyed or hurt, clear your head of any 'punishing' behaviours or tendencies. Banish thoughts such as, 'I'll show them – I won't touch them tonight.' Instead think, 'I've got to talk to them now about this. I might feel uncomfortable but I can't allow this to spill into the bedroom!'

Reaching out

When annoyed or hurt, learn to reach out to your lover rather than pushing them away. Perhaps you withhold intimate behaviour (such as sex) because you are worried about exposing yourself to ridicule. Learn to trust your lover's response rather than assuming that they will push you away – the way you have done to them in the past. Try out the opposite behavioural response.

Alan started with small steps. First he told Elaine that anger was brewing inside him. Next, he tried touching her hand, then holding her, rather than turning his back.

Positive imaging

Choose a favourite image of you and your lover enjoying sex. Keep this image 'ready' to serve as a reminder when you feel annoyed.

Sensual you dreamercise

Alan used this exercise (*see page 32*) to create dream images in which he enjoyed Elaine's openness and emotional warmth. At bedtime he visualized having a sexual dream that was completely contained in pleasure without any distracting thoughts or images. By focussing on such positive images, Alan began to develop the 'halo' effect, spreading better feeling throughout all areas of their relationship.

Related Themes

Finding yourself naked

If this image is accompanied by a feeling of anxiety or fear then you feel exposed in your sexual relationship or possibly your sexual attitudes, practices or orientation. If you feel free and happy during such a dream, it simply reflects your present sexual confidence.

Watching sexual activity or being watched

See page 63 for analysis.

Sex in the bedroom

Sexual dreams that are set in your bedroom are usually related solely to your sex life. The fact that Alan's dream was set in the kitchen indicated that it related more to him as a whole person and his relationship rather than simply his sex life. Analyse the images set in your bedroom to discover your true sexual feelings.

Sex in the bathroom

Dreams set in bathrooms usually represent a desire for change. The presence of rushing water, or the act of plunging into a bath or shower may symbolize the ushering in of a new sexual you, or the need to change something in your present sexual relationship.

Sex in outside buildings

Sexual dreams that take place in buildings 'outside' of the home are different in meaning from dreams set simply 'outside'. Usually they symbolize some sort of shame: the sexual activity is removed from the home and yet contained within another (usually unidentifiable) building. Such a dream reflects your desire to distance yourself from your real feelings, or, alternatively, it highlights a fear you have of facing up to your true desires.

Disgusted by Sex

"I was outside in a grassy area like a park. Everything seemed dirty.
But not dirty in the way you would expect. Instead, everywhere I looked things
seemed to be covered in muddy, earthy slime. I was calling out for my boyfriend,
James, but did not get an answer. I wanted to get out and as I started walking
towards the gates I saw a young couple, partly undressed, kissing and fondling.
I could not help staring, although I knew I should not. When they looked up I told
them they should 'clean up this mess'. It was as though I did not want them to see my
embarrassment for staring so instead I got angry with them. They walked over and
said it was not their mess so I could clean it up if I wanted. This made me even
angrier. I thought, why should I clean up their disgusting mess? By then all the
muddiness seemed focussed where they were. I shouted after them that they should
not have been touching in public. I ran and took off like a bird.
I was flying as hard as I could. I felt that
it would save me from the disgusting state the park was in."

Background and Interpretation

Mary had been seeing James for a year. She had never had high hopes for a pleasurable sex life because of her parents' negative attitude towards sex. Sex in their household was a bad and 'dirty' word. Mary was an only child and as she grew up she longed for siblings. Her mother told her there was 'no chance of that' and the subject was closed. As an adult, Mary understood that her parents' relationship certainly was not 'made in heaven' and that their separate bedrooms spoke volumes about their feelings.

Mary had always felt that she would wait for the 'right' man to have sex with. The man she dated

before James was that man. However, he finished the relationship because of her negative attitudes towards what he saw as quite natural – an active sex life. James had 'inherited' this negative emotional legacy. Mary was inexperienced, and was not enthralled about having sex, but James was attracted to her many other qualities. He was very patient with Mary, and deep down Mary knew she should hang on to him if she was to have a normal life. Unfortunately, though, she could not shed feelings of revulsion after making love.

ANALYSING MARY'S DREAM

The grassy, dirty setting of Mary's dream symbolizes the earthy and sensual meaning behind it. Mary feels as disgusted by this graphic image as she does by sex. Calling out to James and getting no response is a message from her subconscious that she is alone with her feelings – that they are not shared by James. Mary wants to get out of the park, but her subconscious stops her, literally forcing her to view the sexual activities of the young couple. The way she feels she is staring at them when she knows she should not indicates her subconscious fascination with the lovemaking of others. Mary simply cannot admit to herself that it may be a pleasurable experience. It also symbolizes her subconscious wish to be like others. There is a sense that she will learn from the young couple. The couple are partly dressed, suggesting that the protective mechanism of her subconscious is at work: she is spared the shock of full nudity, which she would find hard to face.

Seeing the couple allows her to 'get angry' with them. By attributing the 'dirtiness' to them, when really, of course, it belongs to her, Mary reveals her curiosity about sensual pleasures but her inability to acknowledge her own earthy feelings. Their denial makes Mary even angrier: she is very distressed at being left with this earthiness. She gives them one final scolding before her subconscious shifts focus. Mary flies off looking for escape but actually wins relief from flying – a clear symbol of sexual release. Her inner desires are masked successfully by this image and she loses her anger.

RESOLVING THE ISSUES

Mary awoke from her dream feeling very disturbed. She felt that an inner battle was developing between the past and present. Her upbringing made her negative in her sexual behaviour – for example, withdrawing from James when he made sexual advances, or feeling fear and revulsion during sex if she did not physically withdraw. However, her present happiness at being with James and enjoying many good times together, created a longing to make her sexual attitudes more positive.

Sensual Exercises

Sensual goodness

If you feel sex is dirty, revolting or only for 'bad' people, try this technique. Bring to mind any positive sexual images you can, either from your own experience, or from a film or book; for example, a scene from a romantic movie in which the hero and heroine enjoy a passionate embrace.

Practise associating this positive, pleasurable image with your own feelings. Remind yourself that sex can be like this image – positive, healthy and good.

Throwing out the rubbish messages

Think about the negative voice you have inside your head when it comes to sex. Does it say, 'You

Related Themes

Flying away from a sexual image

You are trying to escape your own sexual impulses or desires. You cannot face up to your own needs or attitudes.

Falling to earth

You feel let down in some way by your sexual partner or your relationship. Plummeting symbolizes loss of control or loss of joy.

Swooping

You are growing sexually and enjoying the pleasures you are tasting.

Soft and creamy pleasant textures

These textures indicate that you revel in hot, passionate sex. You may be enjoying experimenting with oral sex or lovemaking that actively uses your natural sexual lubricants.

Sticky, unpleasant textures

Like Mary's dirty, earthy images, such textures indicate a distaste with your current sexual relationship or a sexual practice you have tried. It may also symbolize a distaste, or sense of guilt, about masturbation.

Watery textures

If water is overwhelming as an image, then you may feel that you are drowning in the sexual demands being made on you. If there is merely a watery 'surface' to the images in your dreams, you may be feeling a little sensitive about your sexual relationship or practices.

Rough, jagged textures

You are angry with yourself or your lover. If the jagged images loom above or around you, perhaps you feel threatened sexually.

shouldn't be enjoying this'? In your mind's eye write these words on a piece of paper. Then mentally scrunch the piece of paper up into a little ball and throw it into a wastebasket.

Freedom from fear

Visualize the 'negative sexual you' as a fearful, shrinking, rejecting, negative figure in a lonely landscape. Remind yourself that you will become as lonely or dissatisfied as your image if you do not open up to a worthy lover. Then visualize the 'you' who has found freedom from fear, who enjoys the sensations of lovemaking. If your fears start to creep back in, bring to mind the second positive image.

Sensual you dreamercise

Mary used this dreamercise (see page 32) to rediscover the positive sexual attitudes that she had repressed.

Lusting for an ex-lover

"I was in a strange, swamp-like place surrounded by lush, tropical plants that seemed to grasp at my clothes. It was not frightening; in fact, I felt quite detached. My clothes became wet and messy from the plants. I came to the edge of the dark blue water and wanted to change clothes. Lying there on the bank was the soft, warm coat my ex-boyfriend Pete used to wear. I wondered why it was there. Then I realized there were only a few threads of my clothes left on me and I felt a bit ashamed – my breasts, bottom and vagina were exposed. I grabbed his coat and put it on. The warm wool rubbed across my nipples. I felt excited even though I was in this swamp. I felt compelled to stroke my nipples and they became hugely engorged. I was rubbing the material of his jacket over and over them. I then carried on moving the soft fabric between my legs. I was really excited and it did not matter that I was alone in the swamp. When I woke up I could not believe what I had dreamed."

Background and Interpretation

Justine and Pete had broken up about nine months before Justine had this dream. They had had a difficult relationship and, although Justine chose to finish it, she still had many conflicting feelings about Pete. He had always been a great, if a little dominant, lover and they had enjoyed passionate lovemaking in a variety of settings. But Pete had also played some emotional games that had damaged Justine's self-esteem. She felt she never knew where she stood with him. After a year of feeling she was on an emotional roller coaster, and receiving lots of pressure from friends, she finally finished the relationship. Justine has had a few dates with other men since then but nothing seems to be going anywhere.

ANALYSING JUSTINE'S DREAM

The strange lush but dark 'swamp-like' dream setting reflects the state of Justine's mind. In waking life she has felt a little depressed and detached emotionally. The plants grasping at her clothes represent different emotions clamouring for attention. Although Justine felt slightly battered by her relationship with Pete, the decision to finish it was tough. That her clothes become messy and wet – literally damaged – symbolizes her sense of being emotionally tattered. When her intimate body parts are exposed, the dream

reveals how exposed she had felt in their relationship. She feels ashamed because she knows she should not have allowed him to treat her so badly.

Getting to the edge of the water and wanting to change clothes indicates that she knows she must change – she must get stronger. But spotting Pete's warm coat draws her back to the

sexual side of their relationship. The qualities of his coat represent the way she saw him. He was 'warm' in a sexual way. Justine is tempted and puts on the coat. Immediately her nipples become erect, symbolizing both sensuality and nurturing. She feels compelled to rub them, indicating the strength of Pete's sexual pull. Her nipples become hugely engorged, symbolizing how much she still lusts after him. She allows her excitement to take over, not worrying that she is alone in the swamp. She knows better but does not care – she still lusts after Pete.

RESOLVING THE ISSUES

Justine was sexually aroused but also puzzled by her dream, which brought home to her the extent of the feelings she still had for Pete. Certainly she missed him sexually. However, she knew she would never go back to him and worried that she needed to move on and stop wasting so much emotional energy on him. She wondered whether the new men she met could tell that underneath she still lusted after her ex and were consequently put off pursuing a relationship with her.

Sensual Exercises

Letting go emotionally

It is important to separate unhappy residual emotions concerning a past relationship and erotic desire for that ex-lover. Visualize the ex-lover. Now duplicate him or her to make twins: one is the erotic ex; the other is the emotional ex. In your mind's eye throw a cover over the emotional ex. Now you can concentrate on memories of pure pleasure: recall the details of your past sensual enjoyment with your erotic ex. Repeat this exercise periodically and you will gradually distance your emotions from the sensual pleasure. To aid you in this process, throw away mementoes, such as photographs, letters and gifts, so that you are not constantly reminded of the rest of your relationship.

Enjoying the erotic past

You learn something more about your sensuality, your likes and your dislikes, from each lover. There is nothing wrong with taking what you have learned from one relationship into the next. You are not bringing your ex-lover into the bedroom, rather, the continually developing 'sensual you'.

Think about the sensual feelings and practices that you discovered with your ex. Now imagine yourself doing these wonderful things with an imaginary lover. This lover may take any form you wish – what is important is that you enjoy the eroticism you have learned in the past.

Sensual pathways dreamercise

Justine used this dreamercise (*see page 34*) to develop her erotic feelings from the past in a positive way. She placed herself at the top of a wonderful path that wound through some exquisite gardens. At the main turning points in the path she imagined an erotic encounter of the sort she used to have with Pete. But this time it was with a mystery lover.

Do You Need to Leave the Past Behind?

If you are anxious about the amount of emotional energy you spend thinking about a past lover, try answering the following five questions. Each question has three optional answers. Score three points for each answer a); score two points for each answer b); and score one point for each answer c).

1 *Do you fantasize about getting back with your ex-lover?*
   a) Yes, frequently
   b) Sometimes
   c) No, it would never work

2 *When in bed with your current lover do you fantasize about your ex?*
   a) Yes, they are in my fantasies
   b) Occasionally they cross my mind
   c) No

3 *What would it be like to see your ex with another lover?*
   a) Terrible
   b) Pretty hard
   c) It would be all right

4 *When your relationship finally broke up, was the experience*
   a) Traumatic?
   b) Pretty awful?
   c) Manageable?

5 *On hearing your 'special song' do you*
   a) Get very emotional?
   b) Get misty-eyed?
   c) Smile softly?

Score 11 to 15:
HIGH ATTACHMENT
You are still very attached to your ex, and this will influence your relationship with your present lover or potential lovers. Try the following exercises: get rid of reminders; give yourself ten minutes ex time a day, that is, think of them for that amount of time and then banish all thought of them at other times; ask friends to remind you of this if you start talking about your ex; recall their annoying habits; avoid places you might see them; go out with friends.

Score 6 to 10:
MODERATE ATTACHMENT
You are probably only vulnerable to the allure of your ex if you see them. They are not on your mind constantly and you should be able to enjoy sex without them entering your fantasies. If you waver, then try any of the exercises above.

Score 1 to 5:
LOW ATTACHMENT
Your ex-lover is history. You have moved on and may find it easy to recall any enjoyable sex you had with them, and to incorporate the erotic techniques you enjoyed together with your present lovemaking.

Guilt over Intense Affair

"I seemed to be stranded in a mountain hideaway in the distant past. I looked out and everything seemed very far below me. There were other people and I started talking to one of the men. He was very attractive in a Latin way. I felt rather excited by the attention he was paying me. He slipped his dark cloak over my shoulders. It was like nothing I had ever seen before with a crimson lining. I felt very special, as though I had been chosen above all the other women. He took a spoon and started to touch me under the cloak. I did not know his name and when I asked him I could not understand what he said. I reached into his trousers and started stroking his penis. It felt extremely large and I asked him how other women 'managed it'. It was really exciting, although I was surprised at myself talking like that. Then the cloak tightened across my chest. His hand and the spoon seemed to be trapped between my legs. I felt suffocated and said I wanted to stop. Then I woke up."

Background and Interpretation

Penny had been married to William for three years when she started working for James. Up to then she would have described her marriage as happy, although at times she had felt a little neglected by William. He rarely complimented her and, as Penny was insecure about her looks, she longed for him to make her feel desirable. Sex, as with many couples, had bubbled along quietly and was not very exciting. Penny adored William but she felt he had allowed sex to become too predictable and was not passionate enough. Penny had always enjoyed living on 'the edge' a little but this had all come to a stop when she married William. When James started flirting with her and described his exciting lifestyle to her, she soon developed a crush. One thing led to another and after a staff evening at a salsa dance class, where James excelled himself whirling everyone around to the pulsating Latin rhythms, Penny fell into bed with him. The affair was short-lived because of Penny's guilt, but it was very intense. James took her to the heights of sexual creativity.

ANALYSING PENNY'S DREAM

The mountain hideaway setting of Penny's dream symbolizes her need at the beginning of the affair to keep her feelings hidden. The mountain reflects the detachment she had sometimes felt from what she had done. This is quite a common feeling when people have acted out of character. That the dream was located in the distant past was a protective mechanism to distance herself from facing squarely what she had done. The attractive 'Latin' man represents James – the man who could salsa. Penny feels excited by his attention, symbolizing the feelings she had during the affair.

The image of the man slipping his cloak around her indicates her belief that the affair with James was almost beyond her control. Guilt is often rationalized in this way. The unusual touching, under the cloak, with a spoon, distances her from responsibility for this sexual behaviour and reflects the way she has tried to distance herself from responsibility for the furtive, secretive sex she enjoyed during the affair. Penny's subconscious conceals her sexual behaviour when she reaches into the man's trousers: everything is done under wraps. Commenting on his 'size', she is surprised by both her enjoyment of her action and that she should talk about his penis. This reaction symbolizes the shock she felt deep down at her behaviour in the affair.

The cloak tightening symbolizes Penny's feelings of guilt. She quite literally felt suffocated by it. His hand becoming trapped reveals Penny's sense that they would be trapped by what they had done.

RESOLVING THE ISSUES

Penny's subconscious is provoking her through the dream imagery to think about her affair differently. She has no choice but to deal with her guilty feelings. If you have had an affair, the range of feelings you experience may be bewildering, ranging from guilt, to anger, to excitement. It is almost always best to tell your partner about the affair as he or she should have the right to choose whether or not to try to work out the issues with you.

Many people hope to sort out their relationship without revealing the affair to their partner but dealing with the anxiety that involves, as Penny tried to do, will not help improve your relationship with them. You may need to re-evaluate your entire relationship as a result but in doing so sensual communication between you may just improve.

Sensual Exercises

Rebuilding sensual communication

If you have lost the ability to express your needs (as Penny had) even within a basically sound relationship then try regaining it by using in turn the three main ways to communicate sensually – non-verbally, pre-verbally, and verbally:

NON-VERBAL COMMUNICATION – Reinvigoration of your sex life can begin with non-verbal messages. Use your hands, lips and other parts of your body to guide your lover to the places you would like caressed, explored or kissed. Let your 'fingers do the talking' in this form of sensual communication.

PRE-VERBAL COMMUNICATION – Early on in a relationship you cannot contain your excitement, and the sighs, murmurs, moans and groans of sexual pleasure guide your lover to the areas of your individual pleasure. As time passes many grow quiet during lovemaking, allowing the sexual flow to go along without active input, depriving their partner of this form of intimate communication. Give non-verbal 'voice' to your feelings during lovemaking to increase your sensual communication with your partner and improve your sexual fulfilment.

VERBAL COMMUNICATION – The use of words allows your lover in on your sensual world explicitly. The words may take many forms. They may reinforce a practice they are already doing well; for example, 'Please don't stop doing that!' They may take the form of a sensual request; for example, 'Please will you touch me here as you've done in the past?' Or they may be a request for guidance around your lover's body; for example, 'Let me know how this feels.' You can also use words to deepen the moment of lovemaking by asking your lover for positive feedback (something Penny had given up on). All of these techniques will help to ensure that you both get what you want out of lovemaking.

Reading your lover's signs and signals

No one should be expected to 'mind read' in a relationship. However, too many lovers fall into the trap of thinking, 'We've been together for so many years, they must know how I feel by now.' Watch for some of the non-verbal forms of communication listed above and try to understand what your partner is feeling both before and during lovemaking. They may behave in a particular way when they are in the mood for love.

For example, a man may shave in the evening when he wants to seduce his partner or he may always put on certain 'mood music' to communicate his desires. If you are not sure if your partner is sending you a pre-sexual message, ask them in a sensual whisper what they are thinking or feeling.

Sensual attention

It feels wonderful to be told that you are fantastic in bed, or beautiful, or that you drive your lover crazy. Never underestimate the power of such sensual attention. Give your lover these love-making compliments and if they do not reciprocate in

the nicest possible way ask them, 'How did I make you feel?' or 'Do I look sexy?' Some lovers require the direct approach, and this can still be achieved with a sexy whisper rather than a demanding tone of voice!

Lover Turned Mother

"I was driving down the road that leads to my mother's house. There was a woman with a very sexy voice on the radio. She got me thinking about sex. I started stroking myself but then I realized I was nearly at my mother's house, so I quickly finished and zipped up my trousers. I felt nervous as I approached my mother's door. I was wondering where my wife was – why wasn't she with me? I rang the bell and then wondered where my key was. A neighbour passed and said, 'Why are you being so silly, just go in!' I pushed open the door and saw that Helen's and my bedroom furniture filled my mother's sitting room. I called out but there was no answer. Then I heard noises and followed them to the kitchen. Helen was there. She turned towards me, as though it were perfectly normal for her to be working in my mother's kitchen. She asked: 'Where have you been?' I felt like a naughty boy. It was as if she knew I'd been masturbating in our car to the woman's voice."

Background and Interpretation

Bill and Helen have been married for four years. Nine months ago Helen gave birth to a daughter, Stephanie. They had always intended that the first few years of their marriage would be spent as a couple, to get their relationship firmly established before having children, and this is what they had done. They had really enjoyed their early child-free years together. They had travelled around the world and made love in every country they visited. All in all these had been sexy, happy years. When Helen became pregnant both felt they were ready for parenthood, and they were both jubilant when Stephanie arrived.

Six weeks after the birth Helen was beginning to feel a little frustrated – she wanted to make love to Bill. He was a loving husband and doting father but he did not seem interested in sex. Helen arranged for her mother-in-law to look after the baby for a couple of evenings, so that she and Bill could enjoy some 'romantic' time together. However, after sharing a candlelit dinner her husband still did not seem interested in sex. Helen could count the number of times they had made love since the birth of the baby on the fingers of one hand. When she tried to talk to Bill he simply said that between

work and the baby he was exhausted. 'Don't worry,' he would say, 'things will get back to normal soon.' What Helen did not realize was

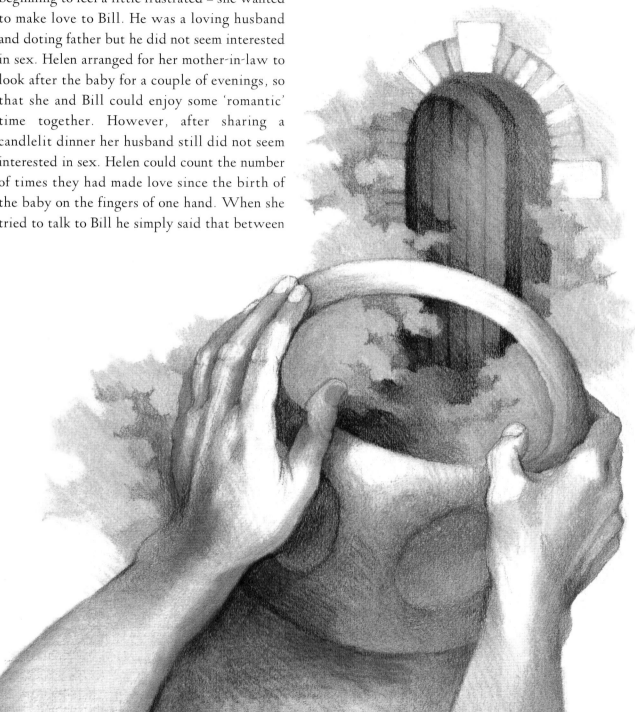

that Bill had felt very differently about her since the baby was born – he put her on a 'motherly' pedestal. Now she was a caring mother, and he did not associate motherhood with sex. Like many men, he simply could not reconcile the mother who nurtured their child with the sexual being he knew his wife to be.

ANALYSING BILL'S DREAM
In his dream Bill hears the sexy voice over the radio – his subconscious is locating sexiness at a safe distance and through 'some other' woman's voice. She is unknown to Bill, so he is able to relax and feel sexy. He enjoys stroking himself, imaging 'sexy' women as he masturbates. He feels nervous as he approaches his mother's door, uncomfortable at having felt sexy so near to home. Wondering where Helen is reveals how completely separate she is from the arousal he has just experienced, and indicates that Helen no longer centres in his sexual thoughts.

Bill fumbles at the door and the neighbour passing tells him not to be silly and to go in, symbolizing how comfortable he actually feels at his mother's. Seeing his own bedroom furniture in his mother's sitting room is the first strong symbol that for Bill sex and motherhood are intertwined – the heart of his

sex life (their bedroom) has been located by his subconscious in his mother's house. This is the source of his inner conflict. Bill calls out and is not answered, revealing how alone he is with his feelings – as yet he has not had the courage to share them with Helen. Finding Helen completely at home in his mother's kitchen and acting like a mother might is the final indication that his feelings about motherhood are linked to his feelings about his wife (who has now become a mother). Bill's feeling naughty symbolizes his guilt about not sharing his feelings with the wife he loves.

RESOLVING THE ISSUES
This dream identified the various feelings Bill had about sex. Once Bill had talked through the dream symbolism he could appreciate that he needed to be honest with Helen so that their relationship was not damaged. Feelings between a couple are dynamic, not static; they change as circumstances change. Very often when a baby arrives, either or both partners may view their relationship differently. Making sure that no one is left in the dark about changed feelings or attitudes and being able to adapt to new situations is important for the continued happiness of both partners.

Sensual Exercises

Renewing sensual feelings
If you have lost 'that loving feeling' for your partner, for whatever reason, it is important to renew the

way you feel. Very often renewing is about remembering sensual moments from the past. Bring to mind erotic images of your lover from earlier days in your relationship. Perhaps you remember a satisfied look under tousled hair that struck you at the time; perhaps you recall a particular occasion early in your relationship when you enjoyed amazing, electrifying sex.

Enhancing sensual contact

Try to ignite new sensual feelings in each other by experiencing your lover's touch in an enhanced way. Try the following exercise. Take it in turns to be blindfolded. When it is your turn, lie back in a comfortable position and enjoy it as they kiss and caress you. Let your imagination run wild with their touch. Experience the wonderful sensations your partner creates for you.

Reshaping sexual attitudes

If your sexual feelings towards your partner have changed as a result of having a baby, try this exercise. Visualize your lover as a sex god or goddess who is there purely for sensual pleasure. Tell yourself that this is a good and special thing. Before you make love hold this image at the forefront of your mind. This will help you to focus on the positive side of lovemaking and to banish any negative attitudes you have developed.

Sensual beginnings dreamercise

Bill used this dreamercise (*see page 33*) to create sensual images of Helen as he was falling asleep. The images would hopefully influence his dreams.

Related Themes

Finding unusual bedroom furnishings in your home

If your dream contains unfamiliar bedroom furnishings, then you are feeling out of touch within your sexual relationship.

Hearing a sexy voice from somewhere in the distance

You are distancing yourself from your true desires. Your subconscious places the voice in the distance so that you can enjoy the sensual effect it has on you in your dream without having to accept responsibility for its presence.

Masturbating while feeling anxious

The occurrence of such an image and associated feeling indicates that you are feeling unhappy about some aspect of your sexual performance. Through masturbation, and the anxiety you experience in your dream, you are placing sexual distance between you and your lover.

Masturbating while feeling great enjoyment

You are enjoying sexual confidence at this point in your life. You feel free to express this as an individual in your dream image.

Resisting Sexual Pressure

"I was in what seemed like a friend's home relaxing. But I didn't recognize anyone. The subject of conversation was a weird table: everyone was talking about it. It had a round, flat top and three large legs that were heavily carved in gothic style. I'd never seen anything like it before. I was lounging practically flat, almost lying on the couch. Then suddenly the table legs started wrapping around my legs. It was frightening. I tried to pull my legs away but couldn't. There was a nightmarish sense of not being able to escape. Everyone else ignored my plight. Then Donna walked in and asked me how I liked the table. I told her I hated it and we had this bizarre conversation about why. Donna said that it was her prized possession and I should like it. We argued, my legs still trapped in the table legs. I refused to agree with Donna and suddenly she dropped the conversation and I woke up."

Background and Interpretation

Henry has been going out with Donna for about two years. He is absolutely crazy about her. Donna has a huge zest for life and lives every moment to the full. Henry had never dated anyone like her before. In their two years together Donna had shown him some unusual sexual practices: Henry had learned about bondage and anal sex, as well as many oral techniques. Henry felt he had realized his erotic potential with her.

Previous girlfriends had complained that sex with Henry was a bit boring and he believed he needed Donna to bring out the experimental side in him. Recently, though, Henry had been

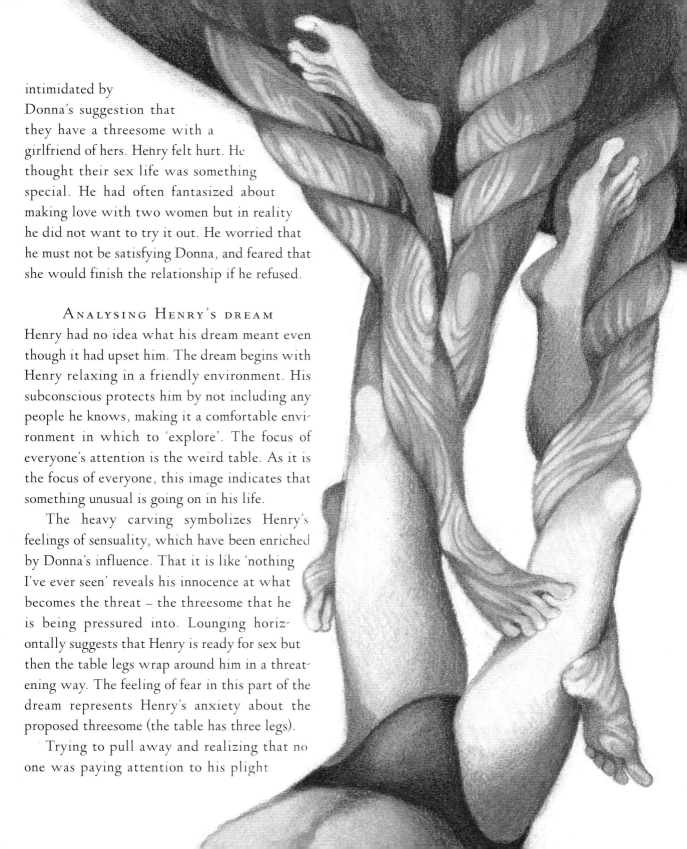

intimidated by Donna's suggestion that they have a threesome with a girlfriend of hers. Henry felt hurt. He thought their sex life was something special. He had often fantasized about making love with two women but in reality he did not want to try it out. He worried that he must not be satisfying Donna, and feared that she would finish the relationship if he refused.

ANALYSING HENRY'S DREAM

Henry had no idea what his dream meant even though it had upset him. The dream begins with Henry relaxing in a friendly environment. His subconscious protects him by not including any people he knows, making it a comfortable environment in which to 'explore'. The focus of everyone's attention is the weird table. As it is the focus of everyone, this image indicates that something unusual is going on in his life.

The heavy carving symbolizes Henry's feelings of sensuality, which have been enriched by Donna's influence. That it is like 'nothing I've ever seen' reveals his innocence at what becomes the threat – the threesome that he is being pressured into. Lounging horizontally suggests that Henry is ready for sex but then the table legs wrap around him in a threatening way. The feeling of fear in this part of the dream represents Henry's anxiety about the proposed threesome (the table has three legs).

Trying to pull away and realizing that no one was paying attention to his plight reveals how isolated Henry feels with his anxiety. Donna then arrives and asks him about the table. The bizarre disagreement directly represents their disagreement over having a threesome. Donna says the table is prized, indicating Henry's knowledge that she places a high value on exotic sexual activity. Throughout the argument Henry's legs remain trapped, reflecting his feeling of being trapped by Donna's demands. The final dream image of Donna giving up on the 'disagreement' is Henry's subconscious reinforcing the message that he can 'stick it out' if he is determined.

RESOLVING THE ISSUES

Henry was unsure how to assert himself in the situation with Donna. He constantly thought about the alternatives but all that mulling over the potential threesome in his mind was doing was feeding his anxiety. As with many sexual problems, the fear of what might happen if he faced the issue directly with Donna was preventing him from saying what he actually felt. His doubts were swirling around without resolution, leading to ever increasing anxiety. Henry's final dream image was a subconscious message to hold his ground.

Sensual Exercises

Sensual alternatives

It is quite common for people to have different expectations about how experimental their sexual relationship should be. When differences arise, finding alternatives that please both people is important. If, for example, one partner wants to take sexual activity into uncharted territory that the other partner finds threatening, substituting fantasy and role play may prove a satisfactory alternative for both. In Henry's and Donna's case, discussing her fantasy in detail may satisfy her desire to experience a threesome, particularly if she is skilled at 'getting into' fantasy talk. In other cases, an alternative may be meeting half way between the partners' expectations. For those prepared to 'walk on the wild side' like Donna, a visit to an adult club, often fetish-based, may satisfy the desire to explore a group environment. Partners may agree to look but

not touch in order to make the experience less threatening. However, no one should *ever* feel coerced into a sexual experience they do not want, at any point in a relationship.

Sensual compromise

Taking turns in pursuing your individual desires is an important part of any sexual relationship. If you can do this successfully, it will make you better able to compromise in your relationship as a whole. For example, one partner may want to work through the positions of the Kama Sutra, while the other gets aroused by making love in different places. Learning to take turns will keep both lovers satisfied.

Your sexual rights

Think through and write down a self-affirmation about your sexual rights (*see page 51*).

Assess Your Resistance to Sexual Pressure

If you feel you are likely to be pressured into a sexual activity that you do not want to try, answer the following five questions. Each question has three optional answers. Score three points for each answer a); score two points for each answer b); and score one point for each answer c).

1 *Would you agree to having sex even when you did not want to?*
   a) Yes, I would
   b) I think there are times that I would
   c) No, I would not

2 *Have you ever tried a sexual practice that disgusted you?*
   a) Yes, and I felt unhappy
   b) No, but I have tried things I felt unsure of
   c) No, I would not

3 *Do you ever have sex when you want affection?*
   a) Yes, frequently
   b) Sometimes, when I would rather just have cuddles
   c) No, because they are two different things

4 *When you lost your virginity did you choose the circumstances?*
   a) No, it was out of my control
   b) To some extent
   c) Yes, definitely

5 *Have you ever felt you could not talk to or express yourself with a lover?*
   a) Yes, frequently
   b) Sometimes
   c) No, I have always expressed my needs

Score 11 to 15:
VULNERABLE TO SEXUAL PRESSURE
Learn to separate a need for affection from having sex. Also, remember that a relationship based on inequality is not worth having. If your lover pressures you to do things that you do not want to do, learn to say No. Make alternative suggestions that you are comfortable with. The more you give in to sexual demands you feel uncomfortable with, the more you become vulnerable in the whole relationship.

Score 6 to 10:
SOME VULNERABILITY TO SEXUAL PRESSURE
You may at times, probably to save an argument, have sex when you do not really want to. Most people go through the motions occasionally to satisfy a partner they love. But never let this response develop into frequently having sex you do not want to have, or feel unhappy about.

Score 1 to 5:
NOT VULNERABLE TO SEXUAL PRESSURE
You express your sexual needs well and will not be pressurized into having sex when you do not want to or carrying out sexual practices that you are unhappy about doing. Maintaining this attitude is important to your self-esteem, so keep asserting yourself in your sexual relationship.

Lust for Hated Boss

"I walked into Mark's office in a very strange outfit: there was no front to my skirt and I was completely exposed. Mark said that we had work to do. He didn't seem to notice my unusual appearance. Then I got up on his desk and spread my legs. He started to examine me as if he were a gynaecologist – he was very business-like. I told him to use a pen to examine me more closely. Mark took a pen and gently pulled open my labia with it. Then I said I wanted to have sex with him. He replied: 'Not until I finish the examination.' I begged him and he put down his pen and buried his head between my legs. The oral sex was fantastic and I was squirming about to get the most out of it. Next thing I knew Mark was on top of me. He was strangely considerate, asking if I was OK on the hard desk. I ignored his question and rolled on top of him. Now we were thrashing about together. It was as if I was on heat and couldn't get enough. When I woke I couldn't believe how sexy I was in the dream."

Background and Interpretation

Elizabeth hated her boss, Mark. He always demanded that things were done his way and never had any patience with colleagues or clients. Elizabeth accepted that she had a good position in a successful company and that everyone had to work hard to keep it that way. Indeed, she enjoyed her work and working hard, and would rather be busy than bored. Her problem with her job was purely to do with the personality of her boss and the way he behaved towards her. Mark did not seem to have any warmth about him and he made her feel

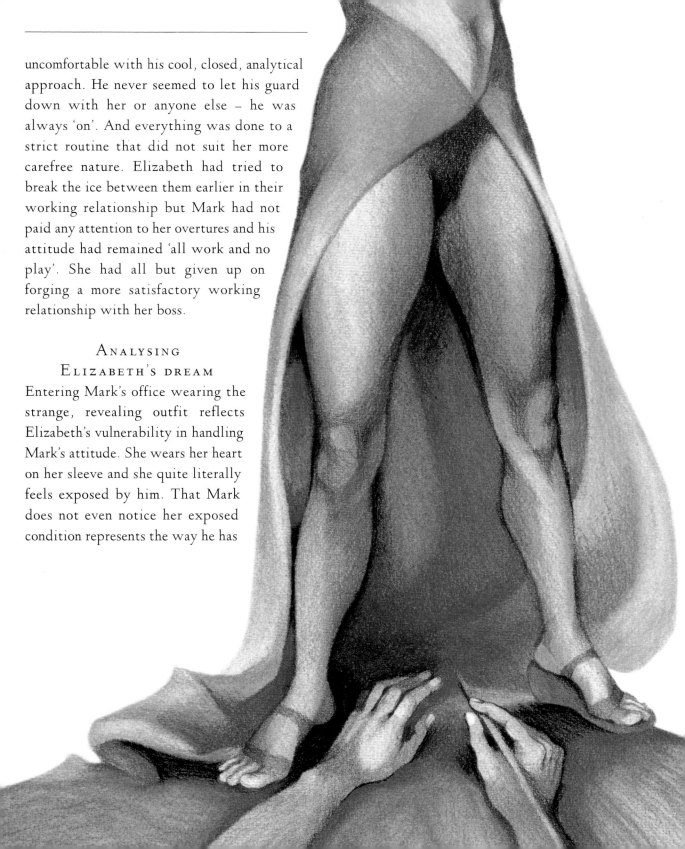

uncomfortable with his cool, closed, analytical approach. He never seemed to let his guard down with her or anyone else – he was always 'on'. And everything was done to a strict routine that did not suit her more carefree nature. Elizabeth had tried to break the ice between them earlier in their working relationship but Mark had not paid any attention to her overtures and his attitude had remained 'all work and no play'. She had all but given up on forging a more satisfactory working relationship with her boss.

ANALYSING ELIZABETH'S DREAM

Entering Mark's office wearing the strange, revealing outfit reflects Elizabeth's vulnerability in handling Mark's attitude. She wears her heart on her sleeve and she quite literally feels exposed by him. That Mark does not even notice her exposed condition represents the way he has ignored all her attempts to improve their working relationship. Saying that he has work to do reflects how he behaves in waking life – all work, even in the face of a half-naked woman. Getting up on to his desk and spreading her legs symbolizes Elizabeth's subconscious desire to get her way with him – she forces intimacy on him. He responds 'like a gynaecologist', again representing Elizabeth's strong feelings that he is not really human, exhibiting no emotional response and never switching off from analytical work mode. Rather than enjoying a woman's genitalia Mark looks upon it as another job to be done.

When Elizabeth tells him to 'use his pen' to examine her more closely, she is indicating her desire to have sex with him. Her subconscious allows her to introduce this idea slowly. Then her true desires are allowed to break through and she says outright that she 'wants to have sex with him'. His answer of 'not until I finish the examination' is her mind providing the negative sort of response he would normally give her at work; that is, work first, play later.

Elizabeth then begs him to have sex with her, and her mind allows him to 'bury his head' between her legs – a most intimate act that begins to fulfil her sexual desires. True wish fulfilment occurs when he climbs on top of her and asks about her comfort. This is the fulfilment of Elizabeth's wish that her boss would be more attentive to her feelings at work. Finally, the thrashing, animal sex they enjoy symbolizes Elizabeth's longing to break out of the straightjacket routine she endures at work.

RESOLVING THE ISSUES

There are many reasons why people have absurd dreams about their bosses or work colleagues. Work takes up a great deal of our daily lives. Our work reflects our feelings of worth and indicates whether we have attained appropriate levels of responsibility in terms of our career expectations. How we feel about our colleagues – the people we often spend more time with than our loved ones – is an important part of this. So it is not surprising that work-related themes feature frequently in our dreams.

Our feelings about our sexual selves are also bound up with our innate sense of worth. The intensity of feelings we have about both work and sex means that dreams concerning work issues often become bound up with sexual images. Usually these images centre on wish fulfilment of some kind but they may also be concerned with performance anxiety. Perhaps the dreamer does secretly find their boss attractive in some way or perhaps they feel anxious about the attitude of their boss towards them. The dream may reflect a wish to get the boss 'on their side'. Or it may reflect a love-hate relationship. Very often intense, negative feelings mask other passions – the dreamer may be attracted to the power and prestige of their boss. Opposites sometimes attract, too.

Exploration of Elizabeth's feelings revealed that she did feel drawn to the power Mark had in his position in the company, and that she was in some way attracted to his cool, controlled nature, which was so very different from her own warm, carefree one.

Sensual Exercises

Dream role play

Frequently, absurd dream images tap into our deeper sexual creativity, so have the confidence to explore and learn from them. One way of doing this is to use your absurd sexual dream images to give you ideas for role play with your lover. Use tact and sensitivity if your dream included people that may cause your lover concern or jealousy!

Elizabeth had fun with her boyfriend, taking turns at role play based on the sexual images she experienced in her dream. She took on the role of the cool, powerful boss and enjoyed telling her lover what to do in the bedroom.

Sensual pathways dreamercise

Elizabeth used this dreamercise (*see page 34*) to develop dreams that she would find sensual. She envisaged wonderful sensual images along her path that included having oral sex performed on her until she 'could not take any more'. She also visualized having exciting sexual encounters in different parts of her office complex.

Related Themes

Coming to work naked

If this dream image is accompanied by a sense of anxiety, then you probably feel vulnerable about your work and you worry that others have noticed. If it is accompanied by a sense of excitement, then it symbolizes a longing for more attention at work, perhaps from someone you are sexually attracted to.

You dominate your boss

This dream image symbolizes a role reversal in terms of wish fulfilment. It may be that the dominant sexual images are more to do with giving you 'power' over your boss than an actual desire to have sex with him or her.

Having sex in full view of colleagues

If accompanied by anxiety, then this image is a strong indication that you feel vulnerable among your colleagues. Perhaps you feel others are undermining your work or talking about you. Exposing yourself in this way reflects those feelings. However, if this image is accompanied by feelings of sensuality or enjoyment it reflects your inner carefree spirit.

Having sneaky sex with a colleague

This may represent feelings of guilt over your secret desire for someone. Your subconscious allows you a little stolen pleasure, although the sneakiness reflects your sense that it is 'not right'.

Sex with a Hollywood Star

"I found myself on a film set. I've never even seen a real one – it was fantastic. There were loads of people. Suddenly I spotted 'Pandora' (a famous actress). She was lounging topless on one of those old-fashioned recliners. She seemed oblivious to everything going on. I was mesmerized by the beauty of her breasts, like firm, creamy custard pies. I felt myself grow erect, and rubbed myself through my trousers. I moved towards her, and she said hello. I told her my name was Eric but she didn't seem interested in that. She grabbed my hand and pulled me down next to her. She placed my hands on her breasts and moved them around. They felt as amazing as they looked. I was getting off on touching them, and they seemed to be growing. We became entwined right there on the recliner in the middle of the set. Pandora was very dominant, telling me what to do: first it was grab her bottom, then stroke her clitoris. I didn't mind – I was on cloud nine trying to keep up with her demands."

Background and Interpretation

Eric had not had a girlfriend for a year and he was the first to admit that he would love to have one. He had stopped mentioning to friends that he would like to meet someone as he felt embarrassed at his lack of success with those to whom he had been introduced. He wondered what was wrong with him, feeling that in reality he was not such a bad catch. He felt he was missing out when he was in his prime – he was fit, willing to experiment and would love to have a satisfying sex life. His sense of failure was starting to make him doubt himself, and Eric was in danger of entering into a negative, self-fulfilling cycle.

ANALYSING ERIC'S DREAM

Finding himself on the big movie set reveals how insignificant Eric feels in the real world. Seeing the film star lying there topless is like a dream come true. This dream image is pure wish-fulfilment on Eric's part. His subconscious is also reflecting the emotional place Eric would like to be: Pandora is oblivious to the world, which is how Eric would love to be rather than feeling needy as he does right now. When Eric

focuses on the film star's 'creamy' breasts, he is revealing two distinct unfulfilled needs. Currently, both his erotic needs and his need to be emotionally nurtured are not being met. When breasts are the focus of an erotic image, and described in an almost comforting way as 'pie-like', they often symbolize the need to be nurtured by a female figure.

Eric's erotic needs immediately take precedence, though, as indicated by Pandora's lack of interest in his name: she does not want to know him personally, she simply wants to be touched by him!

His subconscious shapes the dream around her: she pulls him down next to her and circles his hands over her breasts. This is a strong symbol of Eric's wish to meet a more dominant woman. He fears rejection, so he would love a woman to send out clear messages that she wants him.

Becoming entwined in public symbolizes Eric's desire to be seen to be successful with women. The final images in which the film star is very dominant, directing his every move, continues to reflect his need to be shown directly that a woman wants him. And what better image for his subconscious to conjure up than that of a pampered star who asks for, and generally gets, exactly what she wants.

RESOLVING THE ISSUES

The dream fulfilled some of Eric's erotic needs by allowing him some sexual pleasure. At the same time, the dream indicates that Eric needs to act to rebuild his confidence in himself as a man and potential lover before he will become sexually attractive to others.

If you have been lonely, or suffered some form of sexual or emotional rejection, try the sensual exercises described opposite to rebuild your belief in your sensual self.

Assess Your Passion Potential

To discover how passionate you can be, try answering the following five questions.
Each question has three optional answers. Score three points for each answer a);
score two points for each answer b); and score one point for each answer c).

1 *Have you ever made love in an unusual place or in an unusual way?*
   a) Yes, my lover and I have had some unusual experiences
   b) Some of our lovemaking has been fairly sexy
   c) No, I wouldn't be interested

2 *Has a lover ever shocked you with any erotic suggestions?*
   a) No, even if something didn't appeal to me I wouldn't be shocked
   b) I may have felt uncomfortable sometimes
   c) Yes, I've been shocked by suggestions

3 *How much do you enjoy trying new sexual techniques?*
   a) I love trying new techniques, and am often the one to suggest them
   b) I'm as adventurous as the next person
   c) I prefer to leave things the way they are

4 *Are you willing to describe in detail your sexual desires or needs?*
   a) Yes, I think it's important to say what turns you on
   b) When I feel really confident I do
   c) I could never describe anything in detail

Sensual Exercises

Sensual self-belief through dream images

Take hold of your sensual dream images and use them to remind yourself of how desirable you were in the dream: you can be just as desirable in your waking life. As you relax, recall the images that brought you the most pleasure. Eric recalled Pandora pulling him down as though she had to have him sexually. Relive the episode, going over every detail in your mind. You can have the same sexual confidence in your life if only you can develop sensual self-belief.

Sensual strategies

Use dream images to help you develop new sexual strategies. As your subconscious maps out for you new possibilities, try them in waking life with your lover. Eric, for example, could ask his next lover to 'tell me step-by-step' what she would like, in a sort of role play of discovery, just as Pandora had told him in his dream how to pleasure her. Not only would using this strategy help develop sensual communication, it might be very erotic if Eric and his lover develop it into a role-play theme.

---

5 *How would you feel if your lover bought you something sexy?*
  a) I'd be excited to try it out/on
  b) I'd be happy about it
  c) I'd be embarrassed

Score 11 to 15:
HIGH PASSION POTENTIAL
You enjoy being passionate with your lover and are not frightened to try new things. You feel that keeping the passion alive depends on being open with each other, willing to explore each other's sensuality and not being afraid to say 'No' to something that does not appeal to you.

Score 6 to 10:
MODERATE PASSION POTENTIAL
You have some reservations about opening up to your lover. Do not forget that people want to know when they turn you on, what else they could try to please you and what you like doing to them! Be confident about communicating your needs to your lover. Try some of the sensual exercises designed to help build sexual communication described in relation to Penny's dream case study (*see pages 102–3*), or the sensual exercises designed to help build up trust with your lover (*see page 41*).

Score 1 to 5:
LOW PASSION POTENTIAL
Negative sexual attitudes are undoubtedly holding you back from reaching your full passion potential. Read through the sensual exercises in Mary's dream case study (*see pages 92–5*) to help build positive sexual attitudes. Reach out to your lover in small ways, perhaps by asking them first about the sexual activities they think about. Practise on your own first what you would like to say to your lover.

Just
Good Friends

"I dreamed that I was meeting Dave for a night out. I was rushing to get ready and get over to his house. When I arrived he was wrapped in a towel. I was anxious and told him to hurry up. Once he was dressed I led him into the bedroom, saying we were going to have a great night 'out' (even though we were in). He was hesitant and I was saying 'come here or we'll be late'. The next thing I knew we were on his bed and Dave was taking me from behind 'doggy style'. I was really excited and jabbering on about 'doing it before' and how we'd 'missed so much'. We carried on with Dave banging away like mad – it was very vigorous sex. Dave's flatmate then walked in and said, 'Oh, it's you two', and carried on talking to us as though we were on a regular evening out. Next Dave rolled on to his back and pulled me on top so that I was lying on my back on his chest. I told him I'd never done that before and he asked me, 'So you like it?'"

Background and Interpretation

M elanie had been very close to Dave since they met at college three years before. It was the first time Melanie had had a close male friend. She had never considered Dave attractive sexually but cared very much for him as a friend and spent a lot of time with him. This had caused trouble in her last relationship, as her ex-boyfriend had been quite possessive. He did not think men and women could be 'just friends', and worried that Dave and Melanie secretly fancied each other. Melanie never told Dave about this, as she did not want him to worry about their relationship. Although she could not speak for Dave, Melanie knew that she did not fancy him. Consequently, her erotic dream about him made her feel uncomfortable.

ANALYSING MELANIE'S DREAM

The first dream images find Melanie getting ready as usual to meet Dave. Her subconscious has not yet started throwing up any images that cast doubt on Melanie's real feelings or the meaning behind her dream. Finding Dave in a towel reflects the anxiety she felt when she had to keep explaining her relationship with Dave to her ex-lover. Melanie then feels the need to hurry Dave up, another image from her subconscious representing some anxiety in her feelings: she is restless to get on but her subconscious is saying 'sort out the way you feel first'. Then the dream takes on its apparently absurd twists.

Melanie leading Dave into the bedroom for their 'night out' symbolizes the close bond she feels: she is leading him into the heart of his personal space. Immediately Melanie dreams that they are on the bed with Dave

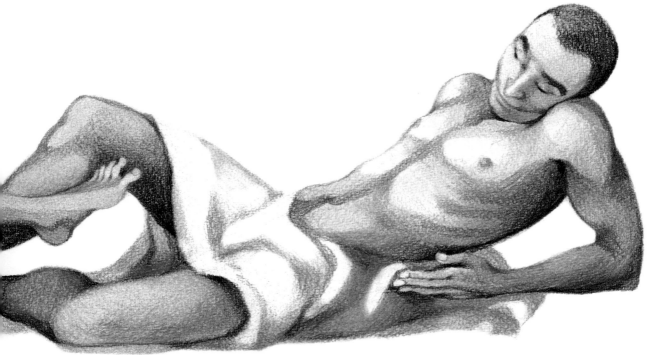

taking her 'doggy style'. This is a protective mechanism by her subconscious. It is easing the emotional load of the possibility suggested by her ex that they could be having sex, by not having them face each other. Melanie 'jabbering on' about not having done this before symbolizes more her need to get really close to Dave than that they should have been having sex. This alludes to the burden she felt in keeping her difficulties with her ex from Dave. Her mind is telling her that she should have shared her deepest troubles. The vigorous sex is due to

her subconscious connecting the depth and 'vigour' of their friendship to the sexual suggestions made by her ex. Our minds often connect different intense feelings and bind them together in dream images. When the flatmate comes in and talks to them matter-of-factly, it indicates that the sex is not really sex, just an intense connection. Dave rolls her onto her back again so they are still not facing each other as they have sex. Talking about never having done this position before is simply her subconscious telling her she has never had such a close friend that there

Are You Sexually Attracted to Your Friend?

To discover your true feelings regarding a close friend of the opposite sex,
answer Yes or No to the following five questions:

1 *Do you get jealous when your friend dates someone?*
YES / NO

2 *Do you fantasize about having sex with your friend?*
YES / NO

3 *Have you ever had sexual contact with your friend, possibly after drinking?*
YES / NO

4 *Has anyone ever commented that you two should really be 'going out'?*
YES / NO

5 *Do you flirt with your friend?*
YES / NO

If you answered 'Yes' to three or more questions, then you may harbour a secret desire for your friend. This number of 'Yes' answers takes you beyond the normal curiosity friends often have about each other. For example, wondering what your friend would be like in bed is common, but if you get jealous when they go out with someone else and have fantasized about them, too, then you probably have deeper feelings than you have been prepared to admit up to now. Ask yourself what is stopping you from being more than friends. Is it fear of losing the friendship if you confess your deeper feelings? Handled tactfully, when sober, you should be able to talk about your feelings without jeopardizing the friendship if your friend does not feel the same.

have been 'difficulties' with. Although Melanie has very deep feelings of friendship for Dave, the sexual images in her dream simply contain messages of the importance of being completely honest with such a close friend.

RESOLVING THE ISSUES

People frequently have erotic dreams about their friends. In some cases, intense feelings of friendly love do ignite sexual desire. Because you find your friend's personality so attractive you may then also harbour feelings of physical attraction. In other cases, as with Melanie, erotic dream images may contain other messages about the friendship. It is important if you do discover feelings for your friend, which you

were not previously aware of, that you examine the context of your friendship and decide whether to let the person know or not.

After careful thought about her dream, Melanie felt confident that she did not harbour a secret desire for Dave. She did decide to be honest with him about all aspects of their friendship, though. This included talking about the difficulties she had had with her ex. It turned out that Dave had had the same problem with a woman he had dated for a few weeks casually – she was always asking questions about his friendship with Melanie. They agreed after talking together that future partners would know that both Dave and Melanie felt the same – and it was friendship only!

Related Themes

Your friend suggesting sex

If, in your dream, you enjoy your friend suggesting that you have sex and then go on to dream of making love together, you are projecting your own feelings onto your friend. Your subconscious has turned the situation around, so that your friend has to make the first moves when, in reality, you would like to.

If these images make you feel anxious, they reveal that your subconscious has detected that your friend has feelings of lust for you, feelings which you do not share.

Trying to get your friend into bed

If you have an intense dream image that you are trying to get your friend to have sex with you, then it is a strong symbol of your basic desires. However, if, as in Melanie's dream, your friend plays an equal part, then the dream imagery is less potent.

Finding your friend in your bed

This is a 'gentle' symbol from your subconscious that you have stronger feelings for your friend than you realize.

Sex at the Football Stadium

"I was at a football game, standing in the middle of a large crowd of fans. We were having a fantastic time as my team were outdoing themselves. Their performance was quite unbelievable and I felt elated. We started chanting at the other team; I felt at home with my fellow fans. The chanting was so intense it was like a thundering in the stands. The next thing I knew, a really attractive woman was cheering next to me. Giving me a naughty grin, she reached across and started stroking my penis through my jeans. 'Isn't this great?' she said.

I didn't know if she meant the game or stroking me. I was saying, 'Yes, yes', and turned to face her head on. I grabbed her buttocks with both hands and lifted her so that she was standing on the bench. We started having sex in this position, facing each other. It felt so good – I can't explain it. I wanted it to go on and on.

I woke up wishing my dream could continue."

Background and Interpretation

Simon was single when he had this dream. He was really enjoying his bachelor life, having come out of an intense five-year relationship six months before. Simon enjoyed going out with friends, flirting with women, having the odd date and generally doing what he wanted when he wanted to. Friends had tried setting him up with other women but these dates had come to nothing as he really did not want a relationship at the moment. However, he did feel a bit sexually frustrated and missed the physical side of a relationship.

ANALYSING SIMON'S DREAM

That Simon's dream is set in the familiar football stands symbolizes how at ease he is with life. His team playing well reflects his enjoyment – he is literally elated in the dream. Simon describes the intensity of the crowd's mood as thunderous. Everyone is cheering, and he is in his element. All these images indicate how comfortable he feels with his life now. Feeling at home in the crowd reveals that he feels happy about his 'crowd' – his friends in waking life.

Do Your Fantasies Enhance Your Sex Life?

Evaluate how confident you are about using your fantasies to enhance your sex life by answering the following five questions. Each question has three optional answers. Score three points for each answer a); score two points for each answer b); and score one point for each answer c).

1 *How frequently do you incorporate something someone has told you (perhaps a sexual encounter) in your fantasy life?*
   a) I frequently find my mind wandering off into a sexy adventure after being told a sexy story by someone
   b) I might do if the story really turned me on
   c) It wouldn't cross my mind

2 *How frequently do you use fantasies during sex?*
   a) I fantasize a lot
   b) Sometimes I fantasize
   c) I never fantasize

3 *Are your fantasies always about the same thing?*
   a) No, I fantasize about all sorts of things
   b) There's some variety
   c) If I fantasize it is always the same

4 *How confident are you about sharing your fantasies with a lover?*
   a) I love describing the juicy details
   b) If they did, I would
   c) I would never talk about sexual fantasies

5 *How would you feel if out of the blue your lover started describing a fantasy?*
   a) I'd feel terribly excited
   b) I'd probably be OK about it
   c) I'd feel threatened

Score 11 to 15 points:
HIGH LEVEL OF FANTASY
You have got into the spirit of things! You realize that your sexual fantasies can enrich your lovemaking. You do not feel guilty about your creative mind and you are not threatened if your lover shares their fantasies with you.

Score 6 to 10 points:
MODERATE LEVEL OF FANTASY
You have some confidence when it comes to your fantasy life but may be missing out on extra fun. If you have not shared a fantasy with your current lover, start by asking them about theirs – have they had one recently? Did it include you? Or ask them if they would like you to describe in delicious detail a recent fantasy of yours. You will probably find you both get sexually aroused telling each other fantasy stories.

Score 1 to 5 points:
LOW LEVEL OF FANTASY
You undoubtedly have negative attitudes about sexual fantasy. There is nothing shameful in using your imagination to give you some sexual pleasure. You may fantasize about making love in an unusual place or position. By sharing such fantasies you and your lover may go on to try new ways of making love. Try some sensual exercises that nurture your sexuality (*see pages 50–51*).

Related Themes

Having sex while wearing sports clothes

If this image is accompanied by anxiety, then your subconscious is linking performance with sex. Sex is about you finding and receiving pleasure. It is not about your performance. Take a step back from your lovemaking and learn to let go. Instead of concentrating on the end result, think of the pleasure while you are indulging in foreplay or making love.

Having sex in an empty sports stadium

The sheer loneliness of such an image symbolizes your anxiety or guilt over a recent sexual encounter or relationship. If, however, it is accompanied by a breathtaking sense of adventure, then it simply reflects your more daring sexual desires.

Having sex in a gym or while using sports equipment

If you dream of unusual sexual activity with various 'equipment' it may mean that you are longing to be more open-minded in your sex life, or wanting to try more unusual sexual practices.

The attractive woman appearing and stroking his penis is pure wish fulfilment. The woman being sexually forward with him represents the one thing that is missing from his life and that he wishes for. When he is unsure if she is asking about the game or stroking his penis, he reveals how his intense feelings of happiness represented by supporting his favourite team have become bound up with his intense sexual feelings. His answer of 'Yes, yes' shows his enthusiasm for everything that's going on. Grabbing her buttocks and having intense face-to-face sex shows how ready Simon would be to have some great sex. Feeling so good and not wanting the dream to stop is a strong indication that Simon's life is great but he would reach ultimate levels of happiness if he also had a woman to make love to passionately.

RESOLVING THE ISSUES

Simon's dream presents strong images of his general satisfaction with his life. As he is a bit sexually frustrated it is no surprise that he has exciting sex with an attractive stranger. Such absurd dreams often represent a mixed bag of feelings, which is why they appear at face value to be absurd. If you have powerful emotions about a particular area of your life, then your subconscious may well link those to powerful sexual feelings by using sexual imagery. Simon thought he might incorporate his exciting images in future sex play with a new lover.

Doing a Striptease

"We were in our local bar — our whole crowd was there along with my partner, Nate. In fact, we seemed to have taken over the place. Nate called for more drinks, saying, 'Where's the waitress gone?' I said, 'Don't worry I can " do bar".' Then I was holding a drinks tray. As I handed out drinks, Nate touched me between my legs. I didn't think it was unusual. He said, 'You're looking good!' I replied, 'You don't know how good!' I was acting like a different person. I climbed on the bar and started a slow strip. Everyone was calling out, 'More, more!' I was bumping and grinding in an extreme fashion. I stripped down to nothing except a belt around my waist. I stood there with my legs open and my hips moving in slow circles. Everyone — even the women — seemed to be reaching up to touch me. I was saying, 'Come on, get it while you can.' I felt exhilarated. I woke up feeling turned on but as I rarely even take my clothes off in front of Nate, it seemed a strange and shocking dream."

Background and Interpretation

Nancy has been with Nate for three years and they are talking about getting married. They enjoy an active sex life in which Nate is more sexually dominant. Nancy has always been a bit shy and is happy to 'go with the sexual flow' that Nate creates. She is not very happy about walking around naked in front of him or using sexual positions in which she feels her body is too exposed. Nate thinks Nancy is beautiful and should be proud of her body. He tells her that if she would only let go then they could share a lot more erotic pleasure.

ANALYSING NANCY'S DREAM

Nancy's dream takes place in a familiar setting in which she feels at ease. She is surrounded by the usual crowd, who seem to take over the whole place, indicating that there are not any strangers around. There is no 'waitress', demonstrating Nancy's subconscious wish to be completely at ease with her surroundings. Then Nancy suggests that she will 'do bar' – something she has never done. This slightly absurd dream image is her subconscious starting to push her forward into the arena of attention.

In her new role – the new her – as waitress, Nate reaches out and touches her. This is a symbol of Nancy's subconscious longing to put herself on show for him. The sexual banter, in which Nate comments that she is looking good and Nancy responds teasingly, again reveals her subconscious desire to be more sexually confident. Stripping from above everyone allows Nancy to be slightly detached from the crowd of friends – this is a protective mechanism. She starts a slow strip, allowing the sexual tension to build. Nancy feels so sexy that in her dream the crowd screams for more. This symbolizes her deep longing to be seen as desirable. Opening her legs with such confidence indicates that she wants to let people see another side of her. Telling the crowd to 'Get it while you can' continues the developing theme of feeling fantastic and in control of her sexual self.

RESOLVING THE ISSUES

Exploration of seemingly absurd sexual dream images may shed light on your sexual self. Nancy's sexual behaviour within her

How Sexually Confident are You?

To discover how sexually confident you are, answer 'Yes' or 'No' to the following five questions:

1 If a lover criticized you in bed would you be able to cope?
YES / NO

2 Are you willing to make the first sexual move in a new relationship?
YES / NO

3 Are you able to enjoy lovemaking that exposes you?
YES / NO

4 Would you ask if you did not understand a sexual request or practice that your lover suggested?
YES / NO

5 I have never stopped a sexual encounter because I did not feel good/sexy enough.
YES / NO

relationship, and the fact that she actually wants to develop more sexual confidence, reveals that, in the context of her feelings the dream images are understandable and not absurd. They serve to expose her sexual potential and the other side of her sexual self, which her shyness conceals. Of course, she does not want to become a stripper, she would simply love, at an inner level, to enjoy complete sexual freedom with Nate.

Sensual Exercises

Describing dream images

Some individuals who lack sexual confidence find it easier to discuss sexual images from their dreams than to describe fantasies. This is because they can distance themselves from their dream images, claiming they are beyond their control. If you find it difficult to talk about your fantasies, then use a sexy dream to open up communication with your lover. You may say, 'I can't believe the dream I had!', as though you are innocent of such thoughts (although, of course, your own mind created it!), before going on to describe the sensual activities that occurred.

Final climax dreamercise

Nancy used this dreamercise (*see page* 35) to visualize surprising Nate with sexually confident behaviour. Relaxed at night, she lay in bed imagining a dream in which she took charge again as she had in her stripping dream. She wanted to get back to that place of sexual release when she fell asleep.

Three or more 'Yes' answers:
HIGH SEXUAL CONFIDENCE
You are sexually confident enough to enjoy your sex life, particularly if you answered 'Yes' to question 1: lovers can often be tactless or critical without cause and if you have the confidence to 'cope' with that, you are doing well. Coping may mean telling them that they are wrong or alternatively accepting criticism that is valid and adjusting your sexual behaviour.

Zero to two 'Yes' answers:
LOW SEXUAL CONFIDENCE
You need to boost your sexual confidence. It is time you believed in yourself enough to express your feelings, needs and desires. Try some self-affirmations every day to boost your confidence generally. Remind yourself of your good qualities. When that negative voice starts in your mind (for example, 'They don't really find me sexy'), replace it with a more positive one. Visualize your sensual self as a goddess/god on a throne surrounded by virile/sexy admirers. Take a few moments every day to repeat this visualization.

Ask your lover what you do best. Receiving a sexual compliment can boost your confidence. Try a trust-building sensual exercise with your lover (*see page* 41). Or develop a surprise technique that will drive your lover wild. Perhaps you can try new mouth techniques while giving oral sex.

Making Love to Teacher

"I found myself back at my old high school where I was never particularly happy. There were loads of students around but no one I knew. I sat down on one of the benches to watch the world go by. Then I saw my old English teacher, Mr Baggs, who had always been nice to me but who had greasy hair. All the students used to call him 'grease-bag'. We started to laugh about the old days. I was honest, and said, 'You weren't good looking but you were nice.' Then out of the blue I told him I used to fancy him. Mr Baggs accepted this and said he'd always wanted to teach me the facts of life. He lifted my shirt and started stroking my breasts. Next we were pulling at each other's clothes. I started kissing him passionately – a penetrating deep kiss, unlike any I've ever done in real life. Rain started to descend like a waterfall. We were drenched, which felt wonderful. By then we were having sex on the bench. Within moments, though, I told him we were finished and got up to go."

Background and Interpretation

Lisa had recently experienced the break-up of a sexual relationship, which had brought back all the feelings of self-doubt that she had last felt when she was at high school. Although fairly academic, Lisa had never enjoyed school as she had always felt unpopular with other students. She was bright and studious, but too quiet to be included by others in shopping trips or sleepovers. Lisa had not had a boyfriend until she went to university. Even then her first few boyfriends had been more like friends than partners and no sexual relationships had developed.

With Jim it had been different. She had lost her virginity to him and had been very happy in the relationship. When they broke up – at Jim's instigation – the cruel truth had emerged that Jim had always found her rather a dull companion because she was so into her work and somewhat unexciting in bed. This news had shattered Lisa, who had thought Jim was as contented in the relationship as she was, and she fell into despair, feeling as low as she had felt during her high school days.

ANALYSING LISA'S DREAM

Set in Lisa's old high school, with all the same details apart from the old students who would have been there at the same time as Lisa, the dream revealed afresh how unhappy she had felt at school. Her school days had been uninspiring and she had felt excluded – that was why there were no familiar faces there.

Sitting down to watch the world go by reinforces the sense of distance between Lisa and what is going on around her. That Mr Baggs is incorporated into the dream symbolizes the connection Lisa felt she had with him when she was at school. Like her, he was kind but not popular, and during her time at school she had empathized with him. Lisa's matter-of-fact revelation about liking him indicates her need to feel accepted – he is an easy target to bond with.

Then her yearning to put the emotional disappointment with Jim right overwhelms her and

she tells the teacher that she fancies him. Mr Baggs, in turn, wants to teach Lisa the 'facts of life' – a clear reference to the fact that Lisa was told by Jim that she was not good in bed: she feels she needs tutoring. The dream image of Mr Baggs fulfils this need. He starts to caress her and, in doing so, he unleashes her deepest erotic feelings, which she wishes she had been able to reveal to Jim.

The passionate kiss represents her breaking free from her uneventful past. The sheets of rain symbolize the washing away of self-doubt and the emergence of erotic yearnings. They make love in this 'wonderful' waterfall. Then Lisa really starts to call the shots. Her subconscious wants to empower her in every aspect of her life, including her sex life, and she abruptly brings the lovemaking to an end.

RESOLVING THE ISSUES

On waking, Lisa tried to banish from her mind what she thought were repulsive images of her having sex with the greasy-haired Mr Baggs. On reflection, though, she came to see how these dream images were bound up with her recent feelings about herself and her sexual relationship with Jim.

She realized that it was time to accept the parts of her life she was happy with and to change the parts that she was not. One aspect she wanted to change was to take more control in her intimate life. She wanted to be able to feel confident enough to take an active sexual role with any future boyfriend rather than the passive role she had taken with Jim.

Sensual Exercises

Seven days of sensual exploration

Taking time to explore your sensuality is something many new couples miss out on. They rush in and jump into a sex life that moves very quickly. This is fine for those who are sexually aware and can ensure their needs are met, but not so good for those who have not explored their sensual selves. Lisa may have enjoyed a fuller and more exciting relationship with Jim if she had had this knowledge.

Agree that the two of you will enjoy a 'slow-burner' build-up over a week without having penetrative sex. Instead, on the first night share a candlelit bath scented with aromatherapy oils – no touching allowed. The second evening, massage each other sensually. Try to discover each other's erotic zones – the special areas where you are most sensitive. The third evening, indulge in sexual banter. Tell each other stories that will excite you. On the fourth evening, try some 'feathering': take it in turns to drizzle massage oil over the other and gently draw the feather through it, up and around your erogenous zones. On the fifth evening, try touching without using your hands. You may use your eyelashes, nose, chest, hips and legs. Glide over each other's bodies, driving each other crazy with these new sensations. The sixth evening feed each other a sensual feast containing aphrodisiac foods. Make a picnic on your sitting-room floor and with your fingers feed each other delicious little goodies that will get your imaginations going. On the last evening, continue the teasing – dress sexily, even stripping for each other. By now the two of you will be desperate to satisfy each other's needs. The week should teach you a lot about yourself and your lover.

Sensual pathways dreamercise

Lisa used this dreamercise (*see page* 34) to enhance her dream life. Lisa imagined her path took her through her favourite park where she enjoyed a number of sensual acts with a mystery lover. The path then led her to a beach where a hot and brilliant sun shone. She sunbathed nude and enjoyed watching others do the same. The waves gently lapped her toes and a lover ravished her in the heat of the sun. She hoped to find these delicious images in her next dream.

Related Themes

Having sex with your first lover

This reflects a need to take a step back. Your subconscious uses the image of your first lover as a signal that events are moving too quickly.

Having sex in the bedroom you grew up in

This indicates a need to return to an earlier time in your life. Something in your present relationship is troubling you.

Having sex in the rain

This symbolizes a new era of discovery. The rain is invigorating and symbolizes the 'fluids' of life. If, though, the experience is unpleasant and accompanied by anxiety, then it symbolizes a sense of guilt over your sexual relationship. You are literally covered with 'dirty' rain that washes over you, drowning you.

Having sex with an authority figure from your past

If you have taken a dominant role in the lovemaking, then this symbolizes a transitional point in your personal development. If your dream image casts you in a submissive role, then it indicates that longstanding sexual vulnerabilities, which you may not have recognized, are still there.

PART THREE

Dream Directory

There are potentially as many erotic dream images as there are dreamers, and it would be an impossible task to provide an exhaustive dream directory of every possible sexual dream image. So I have selected those images that seem to be the most common in dreams with a sexual basis, by which I mean dreams in which you feel sexual tension, release or pleasure: the individual images may or may not be overtly sexual. I have also included possible interpretations for a variety of emotions or feelings that may permeate an imageless dream.

Your dream images provide the starting point for analysing the meaning of your sexual dreams and, although they are important in themselves, you must place them within the overall context of your dream and sex life to arrive at the correct interpretation. For example, two people may both have a dream in which a snake curls around their intimate parts, but the meaning of this image may be completely different for each of them. In the first case, the image is accompanied by a sense of anxiety or dread, so it probably symbolizes that the dreamer is being 'strangled' sexually – feeling threatened and vulnerable. In the second case, the image is accompanied by sensual pleasure, so it probably symbolizes an erotic joy they are experiencing, perhaps from a new lover who has a wonderful 'touch'!

Natural and Environmental Symbolism

The setting of your dream, from mountainous landscape to ancient Greek temple, and the atmosphere permeating your dream, from foggy to bright sunlight, can reveal much about your feelings concerning the activity taking place within it. And often particular animals or birds that appear in your dream carry a pertinent symbolic meaning.

Birds and Animals

BIRDS

HOLDING A BIRD: If you derive pleasure from holding and stroking a bird in your dream, you have a desire for tender lovemaking.

A BIRD PECKING AT YOUR BODY Such an image reflects unhappiness with sex. You may feel put upon by a demanding (pecking) sexual partner.

SWOOPING ON TOP OF, OR ALONG WITH, A BIRD This image symbolizes sexual ecstasy and is not unlike flying on your own in its significance (*see 'Flying Themes', page 145*).

CATS

A slinky feline image symbolizes your enjoyment of your sexual self. It quite literally represents the 'cat who got the cream' – or the woman or man who is sexually satisfied.

BIG CATS

Erotic dream images that incorporate large cats (lions and tigers) indicate that the wilder side of your nature is trying to break free. A frequently cited dream in which big cats appear is one in which the dreamer is pleasuring themselves while being circled by a powerful cat. However, if this image produces anxiety in the dreamer, the big cat may symbolize the partner as a sexual predator; the dreamer as frightened victim.

HORSES

Horses are a common image in erotic dreams. This is undoubtedly due to the enormous sense of power a horse conveys in its movement. As sexual feelings are often very powerful, the horse becomes an ideal 'veiled' image in a sexual dream.

A HORSE THAT BOLTS – see Fiona's dream, page 72.

NUZZLED BY A HORSE – see Fiona's dream, page 72.

RIDING A HORSE – see Fiona's dream, page 72.

STROKING A HORSE – see Fiona's dream, page 72.

THROWN BY A HORSE – see Fiona's dream, page 72.

SNAKES

The sensual, writhing nature of snakes makes them quite common sexual dream images. The snake may be feared within the dream or it may give delicate and sensual pleasure. The meaning is obviously completely different depending on the feelings associated with the image.

FEARFUL SNAKE IMAGE A woman dreaming of a snake that causes her anxiety is undoubtedly being undermined by a fear of sex at some level. It may be that she is anxious about her current partner or it may be that she fears sexual relations generally. A man dreaming of a snake associated with unpleasant feelings may have a 'performance' anxiety.

HOLDING A SNAKE This literally symbolizes holding a man's penis. It may be that you would like to feel and touch a man sexually, or that you have recently touched a man and are recalling this in the dream.

PLEASURABLE SNAKE IMAGE A woman who is enjoying intimate contact with a snake is using the snake to veil her true sexual desires. A man who is dreaming of this image may have 'unexpressed' homosexual longings.

UNUSUAL ANIMAL IMAGES

Sometimes erotic dreams contain images of exotic animals. These 'animals' may be part of the background of a sexual dreamscape, or they may be taking part in the sexual activity. Such exotic images usually reflect a joy of sex and/or a longing to break out into uncharted sexual territory.

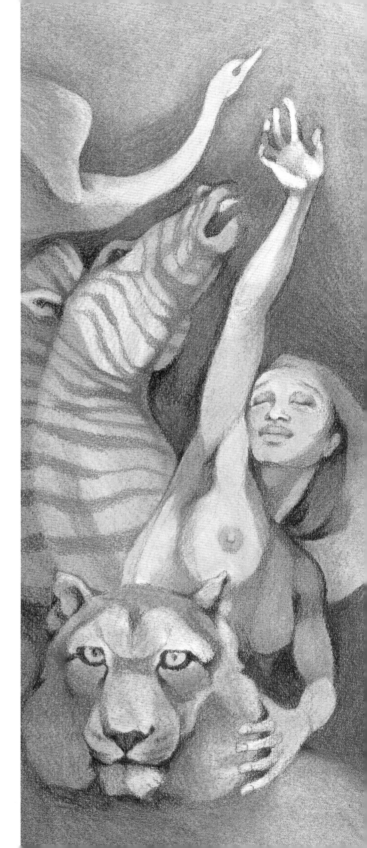

Landscapes

The landscape, or 'dreamscape', forming the backdrop to your sexual dreams contains a wealth of clues to as how you feel about yourself and your relationships at a sexual level.

DESERT LANDSCAPES

The oppressive bleakness of most dreams containing desert landscapes symbolizes a lack of fulfilment in your intimate relationship. The barren landscape, the dryness and heat are frequently accompanied by reports of loneliness or longing by the dreamer.

Very often the dreamer longs to fill up the landscape in order to achieve a sense of being. They search in vain for other signs of life, often finding that everything slows down as they continue their search. The sense of wanting to fill the landscape represents a woman's desire to be literally 'filled' by a man, or, if the dreamer is a man, his desire to literally 'fill up' a woman.

A RECENT BREAK-UP If you have recently separated from your lover, a desert landscape represents the loneliness you are experiencing. It is also an indication of how dulled your senses are as you are not generating a more lively scene. The image could be a sign of depression. Carry out the Sensual you dreamercise described on page 32 to help liven up your conscious life as well as your dream life.

A NEW ROMANTIC AFFAIR Dreaming of a desert may signify that you do not feel as committed to your new lover at a sexual level as you are perhaps pretending to be in your actions. The subconscious often throws up barren landscapes to represent 'barren' feelings. If you are acting out in your sexual relationship feelings other than true sexual desire and the need for intimacy, then you must address

this issue. If your new lover is seeking early signs of commitment from you, a desert dream is a sure sign that you are not ready.

RECALLING A VISIT If you have just returned from a holiday in a hot, dry country your dream could be taken as a literal representation of the local surroundings. However, in recreating the place of your visit, if many details are missing, it may still represent an emptiness at your intimate core.

SEASCAPES

Seascapes can range from thundering waves in the middle of the ocean to gentle tropical sea waters. Generally, seascapes in dreams represent emotion and passion but there are many levels of meaning within that, depending on the type of seascape.

Churning water and splashing waves symbolize turmoil in your intimate life. Possibly you are clashing with your partner and the bedroom has become the battleground. You may be disturbed by your sexual frustration. Calmer waters indicate that your sensual needs are being met. The sense of pleasurable floating that accompanies calm waters indicates satisfaction.

Some seascapes are punctuated by watercraft. Boats may directly represent your intimate relationship or, more discreetly, your feelings or longings. They may also represent the male phallus intruding on to the scene. Plant and animal life below the water often represent submerged feelings. The seascape above is a false cover for feeling overwhelmed, frustrated or angry with your lover.

AN ON-GOING RELATIONSHIP Violent seascapes indicate that you feel overwhelmed by your partner's sexual demands. It may be that you are more sexually repressed than your partner and you see their demands as unreasonable. Being caught up in pounding waves is a frightening experience and a

sign that you need to assert yourself more in your
intimate relationship.

Warm, sensual waters signify enjoyment of your
sex life. This is very positive and you should learn
to prolong your dream for full erotic enjoyment. To
help you do this try practising the Sensual pathways
dreamercise described on page 34.

A NEW ROMANCE A seascape characterized by
much activity suggests that you feel threatened by
your lover. It might be a fear of the unknown – not
knowing what you are getting into. The lovemaking
you are sharing may be moving too quickly for you;
the intimacy your new lover expects may be too
much for you. Waves crashing about, stirring up
turmoil, suggest that you have mixed feelings about
the wisdom of this affair. On the other hand, a
warm, inviting sea suggests that you definitely have
sensual feelings for your new lover. You are not
threatened by the way your affair is progressing.
The timing in this case is obviously right.

FOREST SETTINGS

Dreams of forests tend to represent sexual confusion
or repression. The dark, tangled quality of the
landscape can be quite forbidding. Your
subconscious may be trying to signal to you how
disturbed you feel about sexual longings. People
who dream of forests often feel very guilty about
their sexual desires. These are 'covered up' in the
dream by the dense foliage. Most forest dreams are
accompanied by anxiety. The forest represents the
deeper reaches of the intimate self and can stimulate
almost intolerable feelings of anxiety or fear.
Interpreting such dreams is very important for the
individual. Otherwise they may completely bury
their true sexual self and never experience a
satisfying sex life. They will not be able to learn to
'let go' in lovemaking until they clear a path through
this mass of emotions.

YOUR LOVER WANTS TO TRY NEW SEXUAL POSITIONS When your dream has a forest setting and your partner has been trying to add variety to your sex life, it means that you are fearful of what might be uncovered during lovemaking. It is like opening Pandora's box for you – you know there exist hidden treasures but you feel so guilty about sex, or so unworthy of pleasure, that you hide your desires within a deep, dark forest. This forest may be a direct representation of your lover, ready to engulf you, or a camouflage for your sexual feelings.

YOU ARE CELIBATE Dreaming of forests outside the context of a sexual relationship should be analysed and acted upon. Such forest dreams invariably indicate that you have deep sexual desires that are not being met but which you are fearful of confronting consciously. Many single people do not like to acknowledge their loneliness and sexual frustration. Instead they pretend to the world that they are happy with their status. A forest dream should make you question how fulfilled you are in your current celibate state and whether you are neglecting yourself.

Pleasuring yourself, or masturbation, is often seen as something 'sad' by singles. But your time alone could be a time of sexual growth, a time to explore your body and to find out what sensual pleasures satisfy you the most.

Natural Phenomena

FOGGY/CLOUDY – see Angela's dream, page 48.

RAINING – see Angela's dream, page 48.

SEX IN THE RAIN – see Lisa's dream, page 132.

RIVERS Rushing water is a strong indication of your subconscious sexual desire. The churning, frothing liquid symbolizes both sexual arousal and the bodily fluids that accompany this.

SHIMMERING – see Angela's dream, page 48.

STREAMS A gentle, bubbling stream symbolizes your sexual satiation. People frequently dream of this tranquil image after lovemaking that has satisfied them.

SUNNY/BRIGHT – see Angela's dream, page 48.

THUNDER – see Angela's dream, page 48.

Textures

ROUGH/JAGGED – see Mary's dream, page 92.

SOFT AND CREAMY – see Mary's dream, page 92.

STICKY (UNPLEASANT) – see Mary's dream, page 92.

WATERY – see Mary's dream, page 92.

Buildings

HOUSES

Sexual dreams set within your own home go straight to the heart of your sex life. As your home has not been 'veiled', you may interpret the sex that takes place there literally – whether pleasant or unpleasant, satisfying or unsatisfying.

Sexual images that are set in an 'unknown' home, accompanied by feelings of anxiety, symbolize your sense that you are detached from your real sexual needs. If a sexual dream set in an 'unknown' home is accompanied by a feeling of pleasure, it indicates a desire on your part to be more adventurous – to locate sex elsewhere.

Castles, forts and palaces

The grandness of these settings reveals a desire to take your sexual experiences to another level. They may also symbolize a willingness to try some sexual role play – part of you would like to act out some sexual fantasies.

Nondescript buildings

Sexual images located in nondescript buildings indicate that the acts being dreamt about are of much greater importance than the place they are located. Your subconscious wants you to focus on the specific activities rather than the buildings, which are largely irrelevant.

Buildings with no escape

If in your dream you are trapped in a building and experience sexual feelings of frustration or fear, then the setting symbolizes how trapped you feel in your sexual relationship. If single, it symbolizes how trapped you feel with your sexual feelings or the constraints of your life.

Parts of buildings

Office – see 'work-related' themes in Alan's dream, page 88.

Unusual bedroom – see Bill's dream, page 104.

Closed door Wanting to get through a closed door or hearing sexual noises from behind a closed door usually symbolizes feelings of being shut out by a lover. Alternatively, it can mean that you are refusing to recognize some aspect of your sexual self.

Open door Your subconscious is allowing you to see 'deeper' into your sexual self.

Emotional and *Veiled Sexual Themes*

Many dreams, while not overtly sexual in content, contain symbolism, such as flying or eating, or particular clothes you were wearing, which in fact relate in some way to your sexuality. Some dreams simply leave you with a feeling that they contained a sexual meaning. This section reveals some of these hidden meanings.

Feelings and Sensations

Sometimes dream images can be so muddled, or forgotten so quickly on waking, that you have only a sense of the underlying emotion of a dream. If you intuitively feel on waking that a dream contained sexual overtones and yet you cannot recall any clear images to interpret, use the overriding dream emotion to guide you to make an 'educated' guess at the sexual implications.

BEING 'BURIED' – see Francesca's dream, page 76, for related themes.

ENGULFED OR SWAMPED – see Sandra's dream, page 44, for related themes.

FEELING CALM OR SOOTHED
This sort of feeling in a dream is an indication of the contentment you are experiencing in your sexual relationship or behaviour. Neither do you wish to liven things up nor do you feel guilty or bad about anything you are doing.

FEELING ELECTRIC OR ELATED
Waking up with a feeling of sexual energy indicates that you are at your sexual peak and undoubtedly had a sexual dream. This is either a reflection of the sexual enjoyment you are experiencing in your present relationship or a sign that your 'sexual self' is confident and in tune with your sexual needs.

FEELING FEAR OR ANXIETY
This symbolizes your lack of sexual confidence, either in your relationship or in your sexual self. Sexual dreams characterized by this feeling are a clear message from your subconscious that you are entering territory that is somehow threatening.

FEELING OF REVULSION OR DISGUST
Frequently people wake with an unpleasant 'dirty' feeling from a dream with sexual overtones. This is because so many people harbour deeply negative feelings about their sexual selves. If your dreamscape is characterized by such feelings it reveals that you

are unhappy with your sexual behaviour. This may be either because you have 'gone too far' in terms of what is acceptable sexually for you, or because you have inhibited or negative sexual attitudes.

Flying Themes

Often dreamers recount flying themes that have left them feeling so wonderful they do not want to wake up. The sense of flying symbolizes freedom and release and reflects the release of tension after an orgasmic experience. For more flying themes, see Mary's dream, page 92.

FLYING ACCOMPANIED BY UNFETTERED SEXUAL RELEASE

This symbolizes the sheer pleasure you derive from your sex life. It is potentially a wonderful time for you in your sexual relationship.

SOARING CONFIDENTLY

This reflects your total sexual confidence – you have found your sexual 'wings'. Ensure that you encourage the same in your lover. Sexual enjoyment is enhanced when you both have sexual confidence.

FLYING WITH FEAR OR ANXIETY

This image indicates that you have doubts about your sexual relationship or behaviour. The action of flying reflects the sexual activity but the anxiety reflects your doubt about what you are doing.

Voices

It is quite common for voices to be heard in dreams without an accompanying image. You may not be able to recall what the voices say but you will probably recall the tone in which they say it.

CALLING OUT

A voice that seems to be beckoning to you may symbolize unfulfilled sexual desire. If you are seeking the source of the voice in your dream and experience sexual arousal at the same time, then the unknown voice is a veiled message from your subconscious to initiate some self-discovery.

SCOLDING TONE

This vocal tone, accompanied by sexual activity, reflects how uncomfortable you are with your sexual relationship or feelings. Your subconscious is alerting you to uncomfortable feelings.

SEXY VOICE – see Bill's dream, page 104.

Food and Drink

It is not difficult to make the connection between food, or eating, and sexual pleasure. Nourishment keeps us alive and involves our mouths. Sexual relationships give new life and also involve the intimacy of kissing and oral sex. Food and drink is often incorporated into lovemaking. Lovers feed each other and tease by eating suggestively. So dreams containing food and drink images that also have a sexual basis are common.

FEASTING

Gorging with pleasure represents either a desire for ripe and adventurous sex or deep satisfaction with your sex life. Feasting in a dream symbolizes your voracious appetite for sexual pleasure.

FEEDING YOUR LOVER

This symbolizes your desire to satisfy your lover sexually. The act of placing food in their mouth in a dream image, and nurturing them in this way, is an erotic image, indicating the depth of your love.

FEEDING A STRANGER

This is a potent symbol from your subconscious of your desire to tempt someone into a sexual relationship. Perhaps you have just met someone you find appealing and in the back of your mind you have been thinking of ways to attract them. In your dream you seduce them with the 'food of love'. This is not a bad starting point as people often share a dinner or lunch as a way of getting to know someone as a potential partner.

BEING FED BY SOMEONE ELSE

You are longing to be sexually seduced or, if in a relationship, you would love to be the centre of the lovemaking. Being 'fed' in your dream places you under your lover's influence – they call the shots as you wait for their signs.

BEVERAGE OR FOOD CONTAINERS – see Raj's dream, page 80, for related themes.

IMAGES OF FRUIT

Reaching for some fruit that you cannot pluck symbolizes sexual frustration, either within a relationship or because you are presently without one. If you do manage to pick the fruit, you have sexual freedom or choice. Images of fruit may also symbolize female genitalia – fruitful, lush and ripe – particularly in men's dreams.

Clothing

EROTIC OR SEXY CLOTHING

If you have never worn erotic or sexy clothing in waking life but dream of doing so, and in your dream it gives you pleasure, your subconscious may be urging you to go a bit further in your sexual behaviour. If, however, you feel vulnerable or anxious in the unusual clothing, this dream image reveals some lack of sexual confidence – you feel unhappy at being 'seen' openly to be 'sexual' with such clothes on.

CLOTHING THAT FALLS OFF
If this image is accompanied by fear or anxiety it means that somehow you feel exposed within your sex life.

LACK OF CLOTHING – see 'Nudity', page 150, for related themes.

UNUSUAL ATTIRE – see Serge's dream, page 64, and 'Fetish Items', page 157, for related themes.

BELTS
Belts are common images in sexual dreams (*see Nancy's dream, page 128*). This is undoubtedly because of their 'protective' role in keeping trousers up or pulling dresses together to ensure they are completely closed. In our dreams they symbolize one of the possible hurdles to be overcome before becoming sexually intimate.

BELT FALLING OFF This is a sign that you feel you have lost the opportunity to make choices in your sexual relationship. Perhaps you have been hiding your true feelings from a lover and you worry you are going to be found out. The belt falling off reflects the fear of intimate disclosure.

TIED UP WITH A BELT Your own inhibitions are literally tying you up. Your subconscious has created this image to make you think about how you may be restricting your sexual self.

UNDOING A BELT You long to become intimate with the person whose belt you undo in your dream. Your subconscious allows you to undo their belt, taking you down that path of possibility subconsciously.

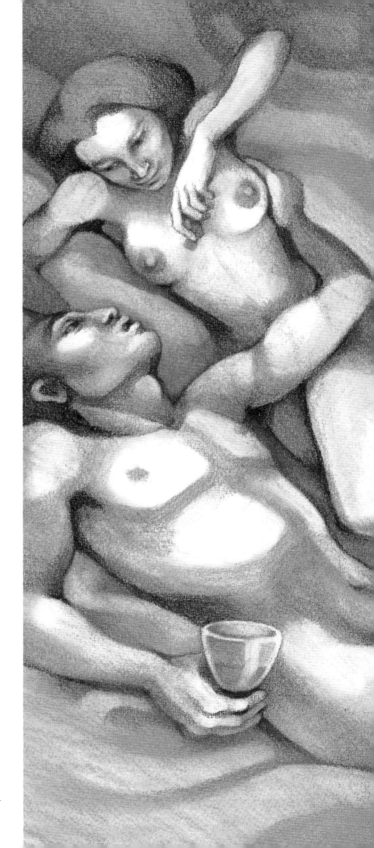

Overtly
Sexual Themes

The presence of certain people in your sexual dreams, and the
exact nature of the sexual activity taking place, can reveal much about your
present sex life or your attitudes to your sexuality. Pay particular attention
to your feelings during such dreams.

Erogenous Zones

It is quite common to dream of a whole person, but less so to focus on one particular erogenous zone. Such selective images are highly symbolic.

FEMALE BREASTS

Breasts in western culture symbolize femininity. They are a very common male dream image as great emphasis is placed on the enjoyment of breasts.

BEING OVERWHELMED BY BREASTS Breasts that suffocate or swamp you in a dream are the antithesis of what we expect and symbolize your distrust of women in general or your present lover in particular.

ENJOYING BREASTS Sensual images focusing on breasts simply reflect the pleasure you receive from them and symbolizes positive sexual enjoyment.

FEMALE GENITALS

Female genitals are a common sexual dream image. Frequently such images are veiled in some way,

owing to the taboo many feel about 'exposing' them to other people.

BEING FASCINATED BY FEMALE GENITALS If you are examining female genitals in a dream image it reveals a natural curiosity. You may long to become more intimate with your sexual partner.

FEMALE GENITALS, VEILED IMAGERY Tropical flowers, plants, decorative vases and receptacles that seem irresistible are frequently experienced veiled images symbolizing female genitals. If you find yourself drawn to, and sexually aroused by, such images, explore how they fit into the rest of your dreamscape. Feeling 'threatened' by such veiled images symbolizes feelings that your lover is too assertive in your relationship.

GIVING ORAL SEX – see 'Orality', page 151.

FEMALE BOTTOM AND LEGS

These dream images are often accompanied by a sense of power. The musculature of the legs and bottom represents the 'power' of your partner, so the feelings that accompany such an image are important. They reveal whether the 'power' is being abused or is giving pleasure.

BEING WRAPPED UP IN YOUR LOVER'S LEGS When accompanied by a sense of anxiety or fear, this image indicates that you feel trapped in your relationship. It may also mean that you are not allowed to express your sexual needs because of the power of the 'legs'. If the image is accompanied by sexual pleasure it reveals how comfortable you are with your lover.

MALE GENITALS

These are included frequently in dreams and are often distorted. If a woman dreams that the genitals are overly large it may indicate that she feels overwhelmed by the demands of her lover. If a man dreams of very small, shrinking or limp genitalia it symbolizes his belief that he is not 'up to it'.

ENJOYING MALE GENITALIA Finding images of a man's genitalia pleasurable or a 'turn on' reveals your contentment with your sexual relationship or your sexual feelings generally.

BEING DISGUSTED BY MALE GENITALIA In a woman this symbolizes negative sexual attitudes, usually of the sort that 'sex is dirty'.

MALE BOTTOM AND LEGS

As with their female counterparts, these usually symbolize sexual strength. If they are clamped tightly around you in your dream, it may indicate that you are being taken advantage of by your lover.

FONDLING OR KISSING MALE BOTTOM AND LEGS Focusing your erotic interest in this way signifies the gentle side of your nature. It may also indicate that you would like to try oral sex but do not have

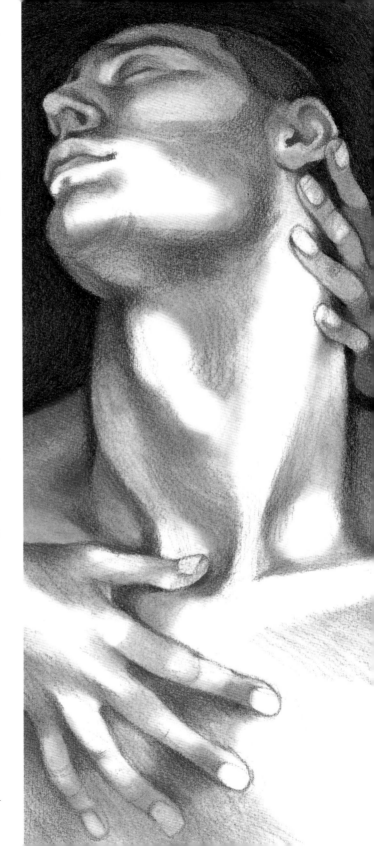

the sexual confidence. Instead you focus on these erogenous zones rather than the penis.

MALE CHEST

Images with a sexual overtone involving the chest usually reveal contentment with your sexual relationship. The chest is 'strong and comforting', and such a dream image may also symbolize the depth of your feelings generally in the relationship.

Masturbation

Images of masturbation are common in sexual dreams. Making yourself and your sexuality the focal point of your dream symbolizes the importance of your sexual attitudes. Your subconscious is creating these images to alert you to this.

BEING CAUGHT MASTURBATING

This symbolizes guilt over your sexual behaviour. Your 'subconscious' attitudes have caught you. It is time to explore your deeper sexual attitudes and ensure that they are not holding you back from experiencing sexual pleasure.

FEELING ANXIETY OR ENJOYMENT – see Bill's dream, page 104.

MUTUAL MASTURBATION

Masturbating in the presence of another person reveals your desire to communicate your sexual needs to your lover. It may also symbolize your sense of independence within your sexual relationship.

MASTURBATING PUBLICLY

If you are enjoying masturbating as people pass by or watch, you probably need to establish your sexual requirements. Perhaps you long to be more honest in your sexual behaviour.

Nudity

FINDING YOURSELF NAKED – see Alan's dream, page 88.

FINDING YOURSELF NAKED IN THE STREET

Feeling sexually aroused in this situation reflects your need for sexual attention. If accompanied by discomfort, this image symbolizes how vulnerable and exposed you feel about your sexual self.

FINDING YOURSELF NAKED IN FRONT OF YOUR LOVER

If this image excites you, then it symbolizes your pleasure at being natural with your lover. If this image fills you with dread, then it indicates the lack of trust between you. Perhaps you need to work on this aspect of your relationship or to find ways to increase your sexual confidence to walk around in the nude.

Sexual Positions

CONTORTED

If an image of yourself in a contorted sexual position is accompanied by enjoyment, then it symbolizes a yearning for excitement – you would literally bend over backwards for some good sex! If the feeling is uncomfortable or one of anxiety, then it may be that your lover is expecting too much from you: your subconscious is creating the message that you have to 'contort' yourself to satisfy your lover.

LOVER BEHIND YOU

This is a clear indication that you cannot quite face up to your sexual relationship. Subconsciously you do not want to have real intimacy, so you do not 'face' your lover in your dream. Alternatively, you may fear intimacy and the image protects you from a more threatening face-to-face sexual encounter.

MISSIONARY POSITION

This reflects an inner need to seek comfort from sex. The missionary position symbolizes a traditional, old-fashioned attitude to sex that is by its very nature non-threatening. If you feel driven to find comfort, ensure that you are not using sex to gain affection as Linda did (*see page* 56).

WOMAN ON TOP

If dreamed by a woman, she is either enjoying, or would like more control in, her sexual relationship. If a man dreams of this image, and it is pleasurable, then it symbolizes his sexual confidence – he is happy to let his lover take control. If he feels anxious in the dream, then he is feeling unable to cope with his part of the sexual relationship.

UNUSUAL POSITION

Finding yourself in an unusual, or almost impossible, sexual position that is exciting symbolizes your desire to seek new sexual activity. If you feel uncomfortable in the dream, then it indicates that you feel under sexual pressure.

LICKING, SUCKING OR NIBBLING – see Jane's dream, page 40.

CLOSED LIPS – see Jane's dream, page 40.

Orality

GIVING ORAL SEX

If a feeling of disgust or anxiety accompanies this image it reveals that you have been, or are being, submissive in your sexual relationship. It may also

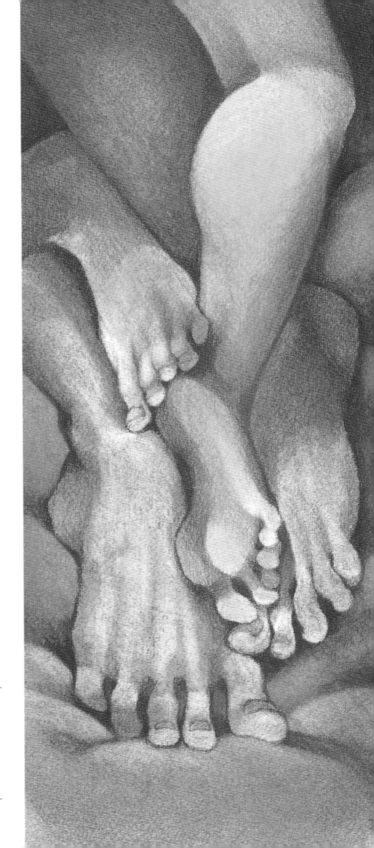

indicate feelings that oral sex is 'dirty' or that you are worried about how to do it to a lover. If the image is pleasurable, it symbolizes your willingness to go 'all the way' to pleasure your lover.

NOT BEING ABLE TO SPEAK OR BREATHE WHILE ENGAGED IN ORAL SEX

This is a strong indication that you feel overwhelmed by your lover's sexual demands or that they are pressuring you to take part in a sexual activity that you are not happy about. Ensure that you feel secure about setting sexual boundaries.

People in Sexual Dreams

FAMILIAR PEOPLE

People find it puzzling how frequently they find familiar faces (postman, shopkeeper, neighbour) in sexual dreams. In some cases these dreams represent wish fulfilment. For example, at some level you may find the postman attractive, even if you do not consciously think about it or put it out of your waking mind. In other cases these dreams represent a jumble of images from waking life: thoughts of sex are linked in your dream to unrelated thoughts of who you recently met or had to do business with.

RELATIONS

People are often shocked by dreams that contain sexual images of their parents, siblings or other close family members. These are in fact common, but of course most people keep quiet about such dreams for fear of being labelled abnormal. It is usually the case that the subconscious has linked strong family feelings to sexual feelings: in waking life the two are most probably entirely separate. These images may also symbolize a natural curiosity about what a family member is 'like' in bed.

STRANGERS OR UNUSUAL PEOPLE

The use of strangers in sexual dreams is usually a protective mechanism. You may long for the sexual activity in the dream but mask who you long to be with by having sex with a stranger. In addition, many erotic dream images contain people who do not speak or are rather ethereal, which adds to the general feeling of arousal. These images exist as part of an overwhelming sensual experience. In such cases, it is important to examine the emotion you felt during the dream – arousal, frustration, anxiety.

BEING TOUCHED INTIMATELY BY OTHERS If this image is accompanied by anxiety then it symbolizes your feelings of vulnerability in your sexual relationship. Otherwise, it reflects a desire for more adventurous sex play with your lover.

FRIENDS

Depending on your need for intimacy, friends play a greater or lesser part in your life. If you are close to your friends, or rely on them emotionally, they are likely to be included in dreams of emotional intensity. Your subconscious may then mix messages and bind two needs together – friendship and sex.

HAVING AN ORGY WITH FRIENDS This symbolizes your intimate bond. The sexual nature of this image suggests your subconscious has linked your intense feelings of friendship to desire for sexual contact, even if in waking life you are not interested in having sex with your friends.

BEING CHASED OR PRESSURED FOR SEX BY A FRIEND This image reflects the sexual cues your subconscious has picked up from your friend. It is likely that your friend is interested in you at a sexual level. (See Melanie's dream, page 120, for related themes.)

AUTHORITY FIGURES

AUTHORITY FIGURE FROM PAST (TEACHER, DOCTOR, ETC.) – see Lisa's dream, page 132.

AN AUTHORITY FIGURE TAKING OVER You cannot face your own sexual longings, so instead you allow an authority figure to guide you through a sexual experience. This is your subconscious allowing you a protective 'distance' from your true feelings.

AN AUTHORITY FIGURE KEEPING YOU PRISONER You have allowed your lover to take over your sexual relationship. You have cast them in the role of authority and have given up responsibility for your sexual enjoyment.

SUBMISSION TO AN AUTHORITY FIGURE If you have pleasurable sex in this way, then it symbolizes your giving in to the submissive side of your character, which may be only part of your sexual nature.

YOU AS AN AUTHORITY FIGURE You may have difficulties accepting your sexual nature. Your subconscious creates this image to give you 'permission' to take charge. It may be time to explore your level of sexual confidence.

Sexual Roles

SEXUAL DOMINATION

TAKING A DOMINANT ROLE IN OVERTLY SEXUAL IMAGES This symbolizes your need or desire to dominate your lover. Perhaps you already do and this image is simply recounting the pleasure you derive from being dominant.

TAKING A DOMINANT ROLE IN VEILED SEXUAL IMAGES You may find yourself being dominant but in the context of a domestic or work issue that at first glance does not appear sexual. However, if you wake up feeling sexually aroused, then your subconscious is to some extent 'protecting' you from your natural impulses.

WATCHING A SCENE OF DOMINATION You may long to take part but your subconscious places you as an 'observer', so that the dream is not too threatening.

SEXUAL SUBMISSION

'SERVING' OTHERS IN A SEXUAL SETTING This symbolizes your submissive side. It may take the form of you 'serving' people who are making love in front of you or of you serving your own lover. Ensure that a lover is not taking advantage of you.

BEING USED SEXUALLY This is a strong indication that you are sexually insecure and you may be vulnerable to letting a lover treat you badly. Particularly if you feel anxious in the dream, or bullied, your subconscious is recreating deep-seated feelings of low self-worth.

ACCEPTING ROUGH SEXUAL TREATMENT This may reflect a part of you that wants to be punished. Perhaps you feel guilty over some sexual behaviour or you feel you are not worthy of good treatment. If you find pleasure in this but do not have low sexual confidence, you may like to role play, using submissive and dominant themes.

Sexual Encounters

EARLY OR FIRST SEXUAL ENCOUNTER

FIRST LOVER – see Lisa's dream, page 132.

REVISITING CHILDHOOD HOME – see Lisa's dream, page 132.

WATCHING YOUR YOUNGER SELF If this image is accompanied by pleasure, it means that you long for the lovemaking of your past. If it is accompanied by anxiety, it reveals that you have not sexually matured and accepted yourself.

THREESOMES

DESIRING OR ASKING FOR ONE This is a symbol that you may want to explore your sexuality, particularly if the third person is the same sex as you. It may also signify a desire to indulge a waking fantasy about the subject or it may simply be wish fulfilment to try something on the sexual edge.

PRESSURE TO HAVE ONE This dream image indicates that you are experiencing sexual pressure in your relationship. It may not literally mean pressure from your lover to have a threesome but pressure to engage in any activity you are not happy about.

ORGIES

PARTICIPATING IN – see Tony's dream, page 60.

WATCHING AN ORGY This symbolizes your feelings of sexual inadequacy. You feel left out of what other people are doing sexually. There may be a sense that your beliefs or behaviour are holding you back from true sexual fulfilment.

INSTIGATING AN ORGY You are at your peak of sexual confidence. You want to take the sexual lead and the orgy scene symbolizes your feeling that you can handle anything.

VOYEURISM

BEING WATCHED – see Tony's dream, page 60.

COMING UPON SOMEONE WATCHING Finding someone else watching people having sex is a wish-fulfilment dream. Your subconscious veils your

desire to watch people having sex by projecting your feelings on to someone else.

SECRETLY WATCHING – see Tony's dream, page 60.

EXHIBITIONISM

STRIPPING IN UNFAMILIAR SURROUNDINGS OR FOR STRANGERS You have sexual desires that are not being met but they are deeply buried. That is why there are no familiar faces in your dream.

SHOWING OFF SEXUALLY If your dream image portrays you as 'flaunting yourself', then it reflects high sexual confidence. Use this knowledge to ensure that your lover feels the same by nurturing them in bed.

SHOWING YOUR GENITALIA TO A CROWD OR STRANGER You are at a stage in your sexual development when you want to cast off inhibitions from the past. You want to experiment and your subconscious is allowing you this freedom.

SHOWING YOUR GENITALIA TO YOUR LOVER
This image symbolizes a readiness to explore your sexual relationship more deeply. You trust your lover and it is time to share your deepest longings with them. Allowing them to explore you in this image may also symbolize a desire on your part for your lover to let go sexually with you.

Sex in Unusual Settings

SPORTS THEMES
Sporting images in sexual dreams are surprisingly common. This is undoubtedly due to the obvious parallel in sports of physical exertion and sweat. Also many people experience strong emotions when involved in a sporting activity similar to the

strength of feeling aroused by sex. The subconscious links these similarities in dream images.

HAVING SEX IN AN EMPTY STADIUM – see Simon's dream, page 127.

HAVING SEX IN A FULL STADIUM If this is an exciting image, then it symbolizes your present enjoyment of your sex life, which you want everyone to know about. If you are frightened by the image, it may reveal your anxiety about what people think of you at a sexual level. Perhaps you are worried about your reputation.

HAVING SEX IN A GYM OR WHILE USING GYM EQUIPMENT If this image is accompanied by sexual pleasure, then it reveals that you are confident of your sexual self. The gym represents 'achievement' and self-care, and reflects sexual confidence. If accompanied by anxiety it may indicate that you are ashamed of your physical self. In this case, your mind has linked showing your physique in the gym with uncomfortable sexual feelings. See Simon's dream, page 124, for related themes.

HAVING SEX WHILE DRESSED IN SPORTS CLOTHES – see Simon's dream, page 124.

TRANSPORT SETTINGS

SEX ON TRAINS Having a sexual experience on a train that is accompanied by anxiety symbolizes your sense of feeling out of control. If the image is accompanied by a sense of pleasure and sexual excitement then it reveals that you are longing to take some sexual risks. If the train itself becomes the central focus of the dream, then it symbolizes your feelings about the male phallus.

SEX IN CARS Feeling cramped or constricted while having sex in a car reflects your sense that your sex

life is unsatisfactory. If the image is accompanied by arousal and pleasure, then it reflects a part of your sexual self that longs to do things a bit differently.

SEX IN BOATS Water coupled with sexual activity is symbolic of your deeply sensual nature. Being washed over by waves while on the boat is symbolic of orgasmic pleasure – you are sexually 'ready'.

SEX ON AEROPLANES Sex in the air usually indicates that you are experiencing pleasure in your sexual relationship or long for such pleasure. The aeroplane symbolizes the male phallus.

SEX AT WORK

COMING TO WORK NAKED – see Elizabeth's dream, page 112.

DOMINATING YOUR BOSS – see Elizabeth's dream, page 112.

BEING DOMINATED BY YOUR BOSS This may simply reflect feelings you have that your boss dominates such an important part of your waking life. Linking this feeling to sexual images signifies how seriously you take your work: both these feelings go to your 'core'. Of course, you may be turned on by power and long for your boss to take you sexually.

HAVING SEX IN FULL VIEW OF OFFICE – see Elizabeth's dream, page 112.

HAVING SNEAKY SEX WITH A COLLEAGUE – see Elizabeth's dream, page 112.

HAVING SEX IN AN EMPTY OFFICE You may simply be linking your feelings about work to feelings about sex. Stolen moments of pleasurable sex in the empty office may be pure wish fulfilment – you would find such a scenario very arousing.

Fetish Items

Fetish images are surprisingly common in dreams. They may fulfil a need in the dreamer that is not being met in waking life, or they may reflect fetish behaviour that they have participated in. Sometimes fetish images take on nightmarish qualities. They loom large over the individual or engulf them. Such images are clearly a sign of guilt over the fetish.

COMING ACROSS FETISH GEAR
You have subconscious desires to either wear, or see your lover in, fetish gear. Your subconscious offers this image for you to explore.

EXAMINING FETISH GEAR
This image symbolizes your natural sexual curiosity. Perhaps you are keeping this curiosity under wraps or perhaps it reflects recent experimentation.

WEARING FETISH GEAR
If this image is accompanied by sexual pleasure, then your subconscious is allowing your wilder desires to come to the fore. If your dream is disturbing, then it symbolizes your negative sexual attitudes – that sex is 'naughty'.

SHOES
Shoes are one of the most common fetish items found in dreams. Being 'walked on' and feeling sexual arousal either serves as a wish-fulfilment dream (you would like to have this experience) or as a sign that you are enjoying taking the role of being walked on in your sexual relationship. If it is accompanied by anxiety, then it may indicate that you feel guilt over your desire to fulfil fetish fantasies or that you are being treated badly in your sexual relationship.

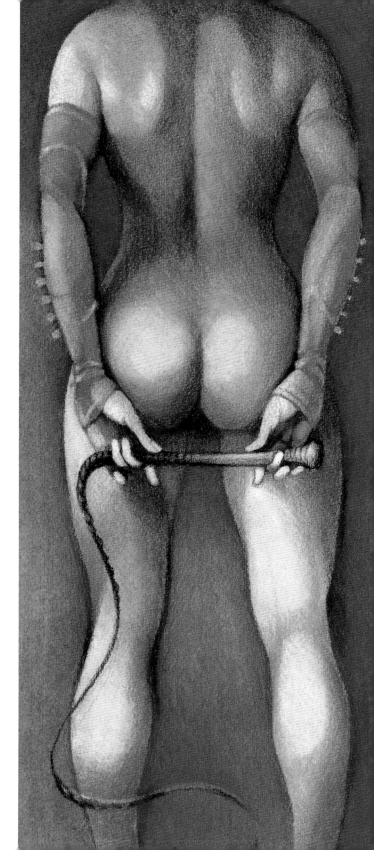

Index

Acknowledgements

Author's acknowledgements

My warmest thanks go to Liz Wheeler for all
her tremendous efforts in making this book happen
the way I envisaged. Jane Laing deserves special
thanks for her exceptional editing. The artist,
Anthea Toorchen, and the designer, Hayley Cove,
have worked incredibly hard to capture the
essence of many fascinating dreams. I appreciate
the understanding of my children, Sam and Stephie,
while I was so busy with the writing. And finally,
this book would never have happened if it hadn't
been for the men and women willing to share their
amazing dreams and stories with me – many thanks
to all of you.

EDDISON • SADD EDITIONS

Commissioning editor Liz Wheeler
Project editor Jane Laing
Proofreader Michele Turney
Indexer Helen Smith
Art director Elaine Partington
Senior art editor Hayley Cove
Mac designer Brazzle Atkins
Production Karyn Claridge, Charles James

The illustrations on pages 53 and 157 were
based on original photographs by Za-Hazzanani
and China Hamilton.